2025 Predictions for Second Half

Psychic Predictions, Volume 2502

26 Psychics

Published by Predictions, 2025.

2025 PREDICTIONS FOR SECOND HALF

First edition. June 22, 2025.

Copyright © 2025 26 Psychics.

ISBN: 979-8231885398

Written by 26 Psychics.

Table of Contents

2025

Predictions For Second Half of 2025

Published June 2025

26 Psychics

I am a skeptic

I have always been a skeptic-the full-strength, "prove it to me or it didn't happen" variety. If someone waved a crystal at me or tried to read my palm, I'd just smile politely and mentally plan my escape route. My future? I figured it was as mysterious and unpredictable as my next haircut (and trust me, that's saying something). The idea that anyone could see what was coming for me? Please. I barely trusted my GPS.

When it came to world events, I was just as hard to impress. I scoffed at horoscopes, rolled my eyes at "psychic predictions," and generally considered myself immune to anything that sounded remotely mystical. That is, until 2008 arrived like a plot twist in a movie I didn't audition for.

Let's hit rewind. I graduated in 1997, bright-eyed and ready to take on New York City-a city where the coffee is strong, the dreams are big, and the rent is even bigger. While Californians were busy inventing the next billion-dollar app, I was determined to conquer Wall Street. I dove into trading stocks and options, and pretty soon, I was living the high life: condo, fancy vacations, and a wardrobe that finally matched my ambition.

Then, 2008 happened. The financial world collapsed faster than my attempt at a souffle. My portfolio? Toast. My condo? Gone. My social calendar? Suddenly wide open. I found myself renting a couch in a friend's apartment, clutching my last cup of real coffee, and wondering if I should have paid more attention to those fortune cookies.

But here's where the adventure really begins. Because sometimes, when everything you thought you knew gets turned upside down, you start to wonder: what if there's more to this prediction business than meets the skeptical eye? What if the universe really does have a few surprises up its sleeve?

It was somewhere between my third glass of cheap wine and my fourth retelling of "where it all went wrong" that Sam-my old friend, fellow crash survivor, and lifelong connoisseur of questionable ideas-decided to introduce me to the world of psychic predictions. Picture us: two financial refugees, marooned on a couch, debating the mysteries of the universe while eating instant noodles straight from the pot. Intrigued? Sure. Convinced? Not even close.

"If these psychics can really see the future," I scoffed, "shouldn't they be sipping champagne on a private island somewhere?" Sam just grinned and shook his head. "Most of them are lucky if they can afford takeout," he said. "And those 'Wall Street psychics'? Please. If they're advising stockbrokers, it's probably on which flavor of Ramen to buy."

Still, that late-night conversation planted a seed. What if there was something to all this-not about whether I'd meet a tall, dark stranger or win the lottery, but about the big stuff? The tides and tremors of the world. Maybe, just maybe, there were patterns in the chaos, clues hidden in plain sight.

The curiosity itched at me, stubborn as a coffee stain on a white shirt. So, in the spirit of scientific inquiry (and with nothing left to lose but my dignity), I decided to dive in. One rainy afternoon, I found myself standing outside a psychic's parlor, umbrella dripping, heart thumping, and wondering if I'd lost my mind or just my sense of direction.

The sign in the window promised "insight, clarity, and a brighter future." At that point, I would have settled for dry socks and a decent cup of coffee. I took a deep breath, squared my shoulders, and stepped inside.

It was like walking onto the set of a movie: velvet curtains, incense thick enough to set off a smoke alarm, and a woman who looked like she'd raided the costume trunk of a traveling circus-scarves, bangles, and enough rings to make Liberace jealous. On the table, a deck of cards fanned out like a magician's trick, and crystals winked at me from the shadows. She greeted me with a smile that said, "I have been expecting you," and motioned for me to sit.

And just like that, my adventure into the world of psychic predictions began.

At first, I'll admit, I was almost impressed. The psychic seemed to know things about my past-my struggles, my ambitions, even a few disappointments that I thought were well-hidden (or at least cleverly disguised behind bad jokes and takeout containers). But as she kept talking, I started to notice a pattern. Her statements were as vague as a weather forecast: "You've faced challenges." (Who hasn't?) "You're searching for something more." (Usually my car keys.) "You've had your heart broken." (Only by the New York Mets.)

She hinted at romantic troubles (news to my happily single self), loneliness (unless you count my houseplants), and career woes (I'd just landed a promotion, thank you very much). Then, with the subtlety of a late-night infomercial, she rolled out the sales pitch: my future was in grave danger unless I purchased her "special" candles and gazed into her "powerful" crystals-each one priced high enough to make even a Wall Street broker clutch their pearls. If I invested in these magical remedies, she promised, my life would transform beyond my wildest, most caffeinated dreams.

I glanced around her living room-cluttered with enough trinkets to open a small museum-and fought the urge to suggest she try her own advice first. My debut in the world of fortune telling ended not with enlightenment, but with disappointment and a skepticism reinforced by steel beams.

But here's the thing about curiosity: it's like a stubborn weed in the sidewalk cracks of your mind. I couldn't help myself. I tried again, this time with a psychic who came highly recommended for her subtlety and, presumably, her lack of candle salesmanship. She was more refined, less "fortune-teller chic," and her approach was more of a gentle nudge than a theatrical performance. She asked questions, dropped hints, and watched my reactions like a hawk at a poker table. Luckily, years of trading had given me a world-class poker face. She fished for clues, but my lips were sealed tighter than my wallet. Her predictions were about as accurate as a weather app in San Francisco. I left with my doubts undiminished and my bank account mercifully untouched.

Most people might have called it quits right there, chalked it up to experience, and moved on to less mysterious hobbies-like competitive jigsaw puzzling or extreme ironing. But not me. If so many people believed in predictions, if entire industries were built on the promise of peeking behind the cosmic curtain, surely there had to be more to the story. Maybe the real magic wasn't in the individual fortunes, but in the patterns that emerged when you listened to a whole chorus of future-seers.

That's when it hit me: to really crack the code of predictions, I needed to look beyond the lone psychic. I needed to explore the collective wisdom-and, let's be honest, the collective folly-of all those daring souls who claimed to see the future. That's where this journey, and this book, truly began.

My curiosity, though battered and bruised, still had a little fight left. I decided to give it one last shot. This time, the experience was different from the moment I walked in. The psychic, a soft-spoken woman with eyes sharp enough to spot a lie from across the room, didn't launch into grand proclamations or try to sell me enchanted trinkets. Instead, she asked a few questions about my past-not fishing for gossip, but genuinely checking facts, as if she were running a background check for the universe. Oddly enough, this appealed to my inner skeptic. It felt almost scientific, and I was willing to play along.

To my surprise, she recounted a handful of incidents that were unique to my life-details I hadn't shared with anyone outside my closest circle (and certainly not on social media). For the first time, I felt a flicker of intrigue. Could there actually be something to this after all? Cautiously, I leaned forward and asked the question that had brought me here in the first place: "So... what about my future?"

Fast forward nearly three years since that fateful visit to Madame Crystal Ball. Looking back, I have to admit-she actually got a few things right. I did take a short-term assignment overseas, just as she predicted (though she failed to mention the questionable street food). Another promotion landed in my lap, and yes, I bought another house-this time with slightly fewer haunted-sounding pipes. She even warned me about an accident, and wouldn't you know it, I ended up in a fender-bender. Not serious, but enough to make me suspicious of every orange cone for months.

Of course, not everything lined up. She promised I'd meet the love of my life within a year. Four years later, I'm still waiting for her to show up-unless she's disguised as my mail carrier and just hasn't said anything yet. Even my most accurate soothsayer was batting less than .500.

But did I stop there? Of course not. Over the next few years, I visited more fortune tellers than I care to admit. I collected predictions like some people collect fridge magnets-some vague, some oddly specific (but conveniently never tied to a date), and most, frankly, about as accurate as my attempts at baking sourdough. The more I searched, the clearer it became: the world of psychic predictions was a patchwork quilt of hopeful guesses, clever observations, and the occasional lucky shot in the dark.

Strangely, I found myself drawn toward numerology and astrology. Not because they were nailing my future (spoiler: they weren't), but because their methods felt almost scientific. There were charts! There were numbers! There was a process, even if the results were about as reliable as a weather forecast for next month's picnic. At least it felt like there was some logic behind the madness.

In the end, no matter how much I wanted to believe, my analytical, fact-loving brain just wouldn't buy it. The idea that anyone could reliably predict the future-especially my future-remained as elusive as a decent parking spot in downtown Manhattan. Fortune telling, at least in my experience, was more art than science, more wishful thinking than revelation.

And yet, I couldn't shake this nagging feeling: what if, hidden in the collective noise of all these predictions, there were patterns worth noticing? If individual prophecies were unreliable, what about the wisdom of the crowd? What if, by gathering and comparing predictions from dozens of different voices, we could find something more meaningful-something that actually pointed, even a little, toward the shape of things to come?

That question became the heartbeat of this whole adventure. It sparked a community, a book, and then a few more books-and now, ten years later, it's a gathering of curious minds who share one thing: a love for exploring this new-age science (or, at the very least, a willingness to laugh at ourselves while we try).

So why am I writing this book? Why would a self-proclaimed skeptic-someone who's spent years side-eyeing every crystal ball and tarot deck-dedicate so much time and energy to exploring what the future might hold? What gives me, of all people, the right to say anything about the next few years-especially after admitting I have zero psychic powers and only slightly more faith in those who do?

Simple: curiosity. Because sometimes, the best adventures start with a question you just can't let go. And if you're reading this, maybe you've got that same itch. So, let's see where this road takes us-one prediction, one pattern, and one wild guess at a time.

The real answer? It's a weird cocktail of stubborn curiosity and sheer persistence (with a dash of "sure, why not?" thrown in for flavor). While I was busy emptying my wallet on online fortune tellers and racking up hours chatting with psychic mediums, I stumbled onto something unexpected. I realized I wasn't just obsessing over my own future anymore. Instead, I started tuning in to what these self-proclaimed seers were saying about the world-politics, disasters, tech breakthroughs, global shake-ups, you name it.

And here's the kicker: while not a single one could tell me anything remotely useful about my love life or whether I'd ever master sourdough, a surprising number seemed to have a sharper sense for the big picture. I started tracking their public predictions-scouring blogs, forums, and the wild west of social media for their bold forecasts about the year ahead. No one was batting a thousand, but I began to notice that certain themes kept popping up. Some predictions-terrorist attacks, tsunamis, political chaos-were echoed by multiple psychics, and, more often than not, the events that made the psychic "greatest hits" list actually happened.

That realization flipped my whole approach on its head. I stopped asking about myself (much to the relief of every psychic within a hundred-mile radius) and started focusing on the world at large. The psychics seemed grateful for the change of subject-suddenly, they were more animated, more willing to share their visions of the future when the topic was global instead of personal. I began collecting and cataloging these predictions, hunting for patterns and overlaps like a detective with a crystal ball.

Of course, I didn't just take everything at face value. I put each prediction through the wringer: Was it plausible? Could it actually happen? A forecast of snow in the Sahara? Fun, but not likely to make the cut. A warning about volcanic activity at Yellowstone? Possible (and mildly terrifying), but it went into the "maybe, but don't panic yet" pile. My mission was to filter out the wild noise and focus on predictions that were both frequently mentioned and at least somewhat reasonable.

This became my not-so-secret sauce: start with skepticism, gather a mountain of predictions, and then filter for plausibility and frequency. I wasn't pretending to have mystical powers or a hot-line to the universe. I was just a curator, sifting through hundreds of visions and prophecies to find the ones that kept popping up-the ones that made you raise an eyebrow and think, "Huh, maybe there's something here."

Before long, I wasn't alone in my quest. A handful of like-minded volunteers joined me, each with their own brand of skepticism and analytical flair. Together, we turned it into a yearly tradition: every December or January, we'd gather the most consistent and plausible predictions and publish them in a book. We kept our lists lean and focused-no end-of-the-world drama, no alien invasions, no "which royal will marry next" nonsense. Just the predictions that were repeated by several independent sources and had a real shot at coming true.

Now, after a decade of doing this, our track record speaks for itself. Our annual lists have hit a success rate of 60 to 70 percent-way higher than any single psychic could ever claim. Think about that: nearly two out of every three predictions we've published have actually come to pass. It's not magic, and it's definitely not mind-reading. It's the power of patterns, the wisdom of crowds, and a big, healthy scoop of skepticism.

Who knew that the secret to seeing the future wasn't in the stars or the cards-but in the patterns hiding in plain sight, just waiting for a curious mind to connect the dots?

And that, dear reader, is exactly why we keep writing these books. Not because we're trying to convert you into a crystal-gazing believer, but because we want to show you what happens when you take predictions, run them through a skeptic's filter, and see what signals are left after the noise has been swept away. The future will always be a bit of a wild card, but sometimes-if you listen closely-you can catch its whispers long before it shouts.

Now, 2025 is a milestone for us. It's not just another lap around the sun; it's a leap forward in both the scale and depth of what we do. Our 2025 flagship edition-The Big Book of Psychic Predictions[1]-hit the presses in December 2024, and, believe it or not, some of the wildest predictions have already started coming true. We flagged March 29th as a day to watch for humanity (and it delivered). We called out the stock market crash in April (sorry about your 401k). We wrote about geopolitics, earthquakes, fires, wars, and even medical breakthroughs-basically, everything but the kitchen sink. Even called out the change in Pope.

But this year, we're upping the ante. For the first time ever, we're releasing a Companion Book to our flagship Big Book of Predictions. It's over fifty interviews of forecasts that touch every corner of the globe. Inside, you'll find everything from the fate of nations and political shakeups to looming wars, natural disasters, and scientific leaps that could change everything. If our pattern-spotting is on point, 2025 (and the years just beyond) are shaping up to be the kind of era historians will talk about for generations.

What's really blown us away this year is the sheer clarity and detail of the visions. The psychics reported "heightened energies" (whatever that means), and their predictions reflected it-sharper, bolder, and more vivid than ever. Most astonishing of all, the number of consistent, overlapping predictions has hit an all-time high. We've never seen so many independent voices echoing the same events and themes. Flip through these pages and you'll see why 2025 and the next five years aren't just another blip on the timeline-they're shaping up to be a turning point in our collective story.

Before you dive headfirst into the future, though, a few friendly disclaimers are in order. While most of the forecasts zero in on 2025

---

1.   https://books2read.com/b/bxOEYo

and 2026, psychic visions don't always respect calendar boundaries. Some events might kick off in one year and wrap up in another-spilling into 2027, or even stretching as far as 2032. We do our best to triangulate timing from multiple sources, but let's be real: exact dates are slippery little things.

And don't forget, geography matters! A "summer" prediction from an Australian psychic could mean December, while a Northern Hemisphere summer is smack in the middle of the year. It's like trying to plan a picnic with a time-traveling weatherman-interpretation is key.

Also, keep in mind that many of these visions are symbolic, open to interpretation, and sometimes overlap across different categories. You'll spot some predictions popping up in more than one section-either because they're just that important, or because the psychics described them in ways that straddled a few lines. We've done our best to clarify, connect the dots, and give you the clearest picture possible.

So, what you're about to read is a blend: direct predictions, our own thoughtful interpretations, and the big-picture themes that emerged from all the noise. The future may not be set in stone, but by weaving these visions together, we hope to sketch out a map-a possible path through the fog.

Ready to see what's coming next? Let's turn the page and find out together.

The Year Ahead-Through a Psychic's Eyes

If you ever want to see the future, start by taking a road trip. That's what I told myself one chilly February morning as I pointed my car toward the foothills of the Rocky Mountains, coffee in hand and GPS set for a little town that barely made the map. I was there to meet Lisa. Lisa was one of the most accurate consultants in our group. She was a normal mother of two - an amateur 'soccer mom' (her words, not mine!). No "Madame" or "Mystic" but who had the highest consistency with others in her predictions for 2025. Her name? Lisa Carter. The kind of name you'd expect to find on a PTA meeting sign-in sheet, not on the lips of people whispering about world events and uncanny foresight.

The drive itself felt like a metaphor for the year ahead: winding, unpredictable, and full of moments where I wondered if I'd taken a wrong turn. The Rockies loomed in the distance, snow-dusted and mysterious, as if daring me to keep going. By the time I pulled up in front of Lisa's cozy, cedar-shingled cottage, I was equal parts anxious and excited-the perfect cocktail for a conversation about the future.

Lisa greeted me at the door with a smile that could melt the last stubborn patches of snow off her front walk. Inside, her place was warm, inviting, and refreshingly free of the usual psychic clichés. No crystal balls, no incense thick enough to set off the smoke alarm-just a couple of well-loved armchairs, a pot of tea, and a stack of notebooks that looked like they'd seen their share of secrets.

We hugged. We have been doing such interviews since 2019 but this was the first time I had visited her home. And since I never spoke about my own future with psychics, I was not a client in the traditional way. "My way of giving something to humanity" - was why Lisa gave these interviews. I was immensely grateful, knowing fully well I couldn't afford Lisa consultation.

After a bit of intro conversations and a few playful minutes with her dog, I settled in, notebook ready, and Lisa poured the tea. "So," I began, "if you had to sum up 2025 in a sentence, what would you say?"

Lisa grinned, stirring her tea with a practiced hand. "That's easy," she said. "2025 is the year the world finally wakes up-and not always in ways we expect."

I raised an eyebrow. "That sounds both promising and mildly terrifying. Care to elaborate?"

She laughed. "Let's just say, if you thought the last few years were a wild ride, buckle up. This year, the big themes are transformation, reckoning, and a whole lot of surprises. But don't worry-I'll walk you through it."

And with that, we dove in-ready to unravel what 2025 has in store, one prediction (and one cup of tea) at a time.

(Lisa is also part of our in-house experts. She reviews all of our final predictions for consistency and ensures we are not including our own internal bias in our books. A lot of the conversations in this book therefore include the results of the over fifty interviews with leading psychics, astrologers and channeled insights that she has reviewed. We remain staunchly committed to our process of honing in on most frequent insights. Interviews were conducted between February and April, so some events may have occurred by the time the book is printed in June end.)

Future of the Wars

L isa poured another cup of tea and leaned back, eyes thoughtful. "If you're asking about the state of wars and military affairs in 2025, the word that comes to mind is turbulence," she began. "There's this sense—almost like a pressure front building across the globe. Military posturing is up, alliances are shifting, and the old rules of engagement are being rewritten. But it's not just about armies lining up on borders. It's more like a chessboard where every piece is in motion, and everyone's waiting to see who makes the next bold move. There's a lot of uncertainty, and that's fueling a kind of global restlessness".

She continued, "What's really interesting this year is how the energy feels different from past cycles of conflict. Yes, there are hot spots and flare-ups, but there's also a deeper current of transformation running underneath. Some spiritual and astrological predictions call this a time of reckoning—a period where abuses of power and old patterns of control are being exposed and challenged. It's not all doom and gloom, though. There's a push toward greater transparency and, believe it or not, a collective yearning for peace—even if we have to wade through a lot of chaos to get there. The military isn't just flexing muscle; it's being forced to adapt, rethink, and sometimes even restrain itself in the face of bigger, more existential questions".

Lisa glanced out the window, watching a hawk circle above the foothills. "If I had to sum it up, I'd say 2025 is a year where the world's military are caught between the old world and the new. There's tension, yes, but also opportunity for realignment. Technology is playing a huge role—think AI, cyber, and new defense systems—but so is the human element: leadership changes, shifting values, and a growing realization that brute force isn't always the answer. The mood is edgy, the stakes are high, and the outcome? Still very much up in the air. But if you listen closely, you'll hear the rumblings of something bigger than just conflict—a global reset in how we think about war, power, and what comes next".

Lisa set her cup down, her gaze drifting to the snowy peaks outside. "What's different about 2025," she mused, "is the sense that the old ways of war are running out of road. There's still plenty of saber-rattling—don't get me wrong—but the energy is shifting. Military leaders and governments are being forced to reckon with new realities: technology is rewriting the playbook, and the public's patience for endless conflict is wearing thin. It feels like the world is teetering between escalation and awakening, with each side trying to outmaneuver the other, not just with firepower, but with information, alliances, and, frankly, a lot of bluffing."

She continued, "Astrologers and spiritual leaders keep talking about this being a 'year of reckoning'—not so much the end of the world as a massive spotlight on abuses of power and old structures that just aren't working anymore. There's a push to expose corruption, to bring honest leadership to the forefront, and to force a kind of global accountability. It's messy, sometimes chaotic, but there's also this undercurrent of hope that maybe, just maybe, the world is ready for a new way of resolving conflict. The military isn't just about tanks and troops anymore—it's about cyber, space, and the battle for hearts and minds".

Lisa paused, then leaned in. "The most fascinating part is how much of this turbulence is tied to bigger cosmic and spiritual cycles. Some astrologers say we're at the start of a rare planetary alignment—a once-in-12,000-year event—that marks the beginning of a new consciousness for humanity. It's like the universe is giving us a nudge, saying, 'Time to evolve.' The turbulence we're seeing in military affairs? It's not just politics—it's part of a much larger transformation. We're moving from an age of brute force to one where adaptability, innovation, and even compassion are strategic assets" 1.

She gave a wry smile. "Of course, that doesn't mean the world suddenly becomes peaceful overnight. There are still plenty of hot spots, and the risk of miscalculation is real. But there's also a sense that the worst-case scenarios—those old prophecies of global destruction—aren't as inevitable as they once seemed. The collective energy is shifting toward solutions, toward finding ways to de-escalate rather than escalate. It's like the world is being tested: can we learn from the past, or are we doomed to repeat it?"

Lisa's tone softened as she finished, "So, if you're looking for a headline for 2025, it's this: turbulence, transformation, and the possibility—just the possibility—of a turning point. The military might still be flexing, but the real power plays are happening in the realms of technology, diplomacy, and consciousness. The future of war is being rewritten, and we're all watching the first draft unfold."

Lisa's expression turned somber as the conversation shifted to the Ukraine-Russia war. "2025 is a year heavy with shadows for Ukraine," she began quietly. "The conflict that started with such fire and fury has become a grinding, relentless struggle. There's a sense of exhaustion on both sides, but also a dangerous stubbornness. Early in the year, especially around March and April, the energies point to escalations—renewed offensives, more destruction, and a growing sense that neither side is willing to back down. Civilians are caught in the crossfire, and the world's attention, while still present, feels more fragmented than before. It's a dark, tense atmosphere, with the threat of sudden flare-ups always looming".

She leaned forward, voice low. "I see a critical moment in late August and September 2025. There's a spike in violence, particularly from the north, possibly involving Belarus. It's as if the war tries to reinvent itself, hoping for a breakthrough, but instead, it just deepens the wounds. There are talks of ceasefires—some even signed—but none of them hold for long. The front lines shift, but the suffering doesn't. The psychic landscape is filled with anxiety, uncertainty, and a gnawing fear that the conflict could spiral out of control, especially as winter approaches".

Lisa paused, letting the weight of her words settle. "But here's what's different this year: the sense that the world is on the brink of something bigger. The planetary alignments in 2025—especially around March 29th and again in late summer—suggest a period of reckoning, not just for Ukraine and Russia, but for the entire region. There's talk of new alliances, unexpected diplomatic moves, and even the possibility of a broader peace summit. Yet, every step forward seems to come with two steps back. The psychic consensus is that while there's no full-scale World War III, the danger of miscalculation and escalation is very real through the end of 2025".

She looked out the window, searching for hope. "And yet, as bleak as it seems, I keep seeing glimmers of light beyond the turmoil. By early 2026, there's a shift—a kind of collective fatigue that finally pushes leaders to the table. It's not a grand peace, but rather a series of small, hard-won truces. Crimea's status becomes a bargaining chip, and while Ukraine may have to make painful concessions, there's a sense that the worst violence begins to subside. The psychic threads suggest the conflict doesn't truly end, but it transforms—less about territory, more about rebuilding, healing, and redefining what victory even means".

Lisa's voice softened. "So, if you're looking for hope, it's this: 2025 is a crucible, a year when everything feels like it's teetering on the edge. But by the time we reach 2026 and beyond, the energies shift toward reconciliation, reconstruction, and, slowly, the return of hope. The scars will be deep, but the spirit of the people—on both sides—proves stronger than anyone expected. The tunnel is long, but there is light at the end, and it grows brighter with every hard lesson learned."

Lisa's tone grew serious as I asked the question everyone wants answered: "So, when does the Russia-Ukraine war actually end? Is there a clear finish line, or are we stuck in this endless cycle?" She took a deep breath, her gaze steady. "The honest answer is: there's no single, neat ending—at least not in 2025. Most visions, whether psychic or astrological, point to a grinding conflict that lingers well into 2026, maybe even beyond. The most consistent theme is a 'frozen' or 'fragmented' peace. There's talk of a major ceasefire or an uneasy truce—possibly as early as late 2025 or the first half of 2026—but it's not the fairy-tale ending anyone's hoping for. Instead, it's a patchwork: parts of Ukraine stabilize, other regions remain contested, and the threat of flare-ups never fully disappears."

She continued, "One option that keeps coming up in predictions is a deal where Crimea is officially ceded to Russia. It's not popular in Ukraine, but several psychics and astrologers mention it as the linchpin for any real progress. There's also a prediction where the fighting simply burns itself out—exhaustion on both sides, mounting international pressure, and a collective realization that nobody can win outright. In this version, the war doesn't end with a bang, but with a slow, reluctant fade. The borders might shift, but the deeper wounds and rivalries remain."

Lisa glanced at her notes, then added, "Another possibility is the so-called 'Belarus option'—a flare-up or renewed offensive from the north, maybe in late 2025 or early 2026. This could force a new round of negotiations, especially if it threatens to spiral into something bigger. The psychic consensus is that while there's no World War III, the risk of escalation is real until at least the end of 2026. After that, the energy shifts: the war transforms from open conflict to a long, messy period of rebuilding, political maneuvering, and low-level skirmishes."

She leaned forward, her voice softer. "A few more optimistic visions suggest that by 2027, we could see the beginnings of a genuine peace process—one that's international, multi-layered, and focused on reconstruction and reconciliation. This would require new leadership, both in Russia and Ukraine, and a shift in global attitudes. It's not guaranteed, but the seeds are there. The most hopeful predictions see 2028 and beyond as a time of healing and cautious optimism, with Ukraine slowly regaining its footing and Russia turning inward to face its own challenges."

Lisa finished, "So, to sum up: the end isn't a date circled on the calendar. It's a process—a series of uneasy truces, shifting alliances, and gradual steps toward something that looks like peace. The options range from a cold, divided settlement to a hard-won reconciliation, but either way, 2025 is just the beginning of the end—not the end itself. The real story will play out over years, not months, and the world will be watching every step of the way."

Lisa offered a gentle smile as we wrapped up the Russia-Ukraine discussion. "Despite all the darkness, I truly believe the seeds of peace are being planted—even if they take time to sprout. The resilience and hope I sense in the people, and the gradual shift in global consciousness, suggest that the end of this conflict, while messy and imperfect, will ultimately lead to new beginnings and a slow but steady healing. History shows us that even the deepest wounds can become the source of unexpected strength."

I nodded, letting that hope linger for a moment before shifting gears. "Lisa, can we talk about another region that's been on everyone's mind? What about Gaza and Israel—what do you see for 2025?"

Lisa's expression grew thoughtful. "The energy around Gaza and Israel in 2025 is heavy—there's a sense of deep fatigue and frustration on all sides. Early in the year, I see continued clashes and a series of failed ceasefire attempts. The conflict feels stuck, almost as if everyone is holding their breath, waiting for something to break the cycle. There's a lot of international attention, but the diplomatic efforts seem to stall, with neither side ready to make the concessions needed for lasting peace."

I pressed, "Is there any sign of a breakthrough, or is it just more of the same?"

She nodded slowly. "There are glimmers of hope, especially as the year progresses. Around late summer and into the fall, I sense a shift—perhaps a new mediator steps in, or there's a change in leadership or public sentiment that opens the door to dialogue. It's not a dramatic resolution, but there are small steps: humanitarian corridors, prisoner exchanges, and some easing of blockades. The psychic consensus is that while the situation remains fragile, there's a growing recognition—both locally and globally—that endless conflict isn't sustainable."

Curious, I asked, "And what about the people on the ground? Is there any relief for them?"

Lisa's tone softened. "Yes, and that's where the light comes in. By the end of 2025, I see more grassroots efforts—community leaders, aid organizations, and even ordinary citizens—pushing for peace and rebuilding. It's slow, and setbacks are inevitable, but the energy shifts from pure survival to cautious optimism. The region's story is far from over, but 2025 marks the beginning of a new chapter—one where hope, however fragile, starts to take root."

I said,"Lisa, I've been hearing some wild predictions about the future of Gaza and Israel. Some say the two-state solution is dead and that Gaza could actually be absorbed into Israel. Is there any truth to that in what you're seeing?"

Lisa replied, slightly concerned, "You know, that's exactly the direction a lot of the big psychic and intuitive predictions are pointing. Many, including I, see a deal, probably brokered by the U.S. and Israel, where Gaza is essentially absorbed into Israel. The twist? Palestinians in Gaza might be relocated—not just within the region, but possibly to places like Jordan, Egypt, or even Saudi Arabia, maybe with financial incentives or international agreements to smooth the process. It's not easy."

"So", I asked, "That's a huge shift. Does this mean the whole two-state solution idea is just gone?"

Lisa continued with the frown, "According to these predictions, yes. That's what I see as well. Pretty clear that the two-state solution is "untenable." The vision is that the conflict resolves not by creating a new Palestinian state, but through territorial consolidation—Israel taking over Gaza, and the Palestinian population being resettled elsewhere. It's a dramatic, controversial scenario, and if it happens, it would completely reshape the political landscape of the Middle East."

I abruptly cut her, "That sounds like it would have massive consequences. Is there any sense of how or when this might unfold?"

Lisa replied, "The timing is a bit fuzzy, but the psychic consensus is that this is part of a broader wave of realignment in the region, possibly tied to major U.S. diplomatic moves and a period of heightened military and proxy conflict. There's talk of sudden, unexpected events in the Middle East—so the change could be abrupt, not gradual. And while it's a bold prediction, it's showing up across several independent sources, which is why it's getting so much attention from those tracking these forecasts."

"Lisa, with all the tension in the Middle East, do you think the Gaza-Israel conflict is going to expand? Or are we looking at more of the same?", I asked - frantically making notes. Loss of the ability to use technology and my lack of habit of making physical notes meant I had to hold up my hand to slow Lisa as she spoke, much to her amusement. I was immensely grateful she was patient.

"That's a great—and tough—question. The predictions I have seen for 2025 point to a definite risk of escalation. There's a strong sense that Israel, with U.S. backing, is preparing for a major strike on Iranian nuclear facilities—using those infamous "bunker-busting bombs." If that happens, it's not just a local flare-up; it's the kind of action that could send shockwaves through the whole region. Some psychics even describe it as a sudden, unexpected military event—something that catches the world off guard and ramps up the stakes overnight."

My pen stopped when I thought of implications. "So, if Israel hits Iran, does that mean we're looking at a full-blown regional war?"

Lisa replied, "Not quite World War III, but the risk of a broader conflict is real. The predictions talk about proxy wars heating up—think Iran-backed groups like Hezbollah getting more active, and the U.S. being reluctantly drawn in, even if it tries to keep its distance. Late 2025 is described as a "rough" phase for the Middle East, with instability sticking around for a while. It's not just Israel and Gaza anymore; it's a whole web of alliances and rivalries that could get pulled into the fray."

"That sounds pretty grim. Is there any hope for de-escalation or peace?"

Lisa replied, "Actually, yes—though it won't be easy. The visions suggest that by late 2025, we'll start to see more grassroots and community-led efforts to rebuild and push for peace. It's fragile, and there will be setbacks, but public sentiment in both Israel and Palestine is expected to shift toward cautious optimism. People are just tired of endless conflict. Humanitarian initiatives, prisoner exchanges, and small steps toward dialogue are all on the table. The timeline is blurry—some of these efforts might spill into 2026 or even 2027—but the energy is moving toward slow, hard-won progress rather than total collapse. And astrologically, the rare planetary alignments in March 2025 are said to act as a catalyst for this reckoning and potential realignment in the region."

"So, we're in for a rocky ride, but not without some light at the end of the tunnel?"

"Exactly. The next year or two could be turbulent, but the seeds for something better are being planted—even if it takes time for them to grow. The future's not set in stone, but the patterns suggest we're moving, however slowly, toward a new chapter."

I was interested in timing, "Lisa, you mentioned heightened tensions in the Middle East through 2025. Can you pinpoint when things might escalate or shift? Any specific months or triggers to watch?"

I could see Lisa wasn't comfortable with these predictions so I wanted to complete this section and move on. I mentally made a note that I won't ask anything else.

Lisa replied, "Absolutely. Let's break it down month by month, based on the patterns I have seen. March 2025 is a critical starting point. Astrologers and psychics both highlight the rare six-planet conjunction in Pisces on March 29 —Saturn's shift into Pisces, paired with a solar eclipse. This energy often correlates with seismic geopolitical moves. I'd watch for sudden military actions or diplomatic gambits around these months."

"So March is the spark. What comes next?"

"Late June to September 2025 stands out. Multiple predictions point to a "sudden and unexpected" military event in this window—likely Israel striking Iranian nuclear facilities. Saturn's tense aspect to Mars during this period suggests calculated aggression, not impulsive strikes. If it happens, expect immediate regional fallout: Hezbollah retaliating from Lebanon, Houthi drone attacks in the Red Sea, and U.S. warships being drawn into the fray despite efforts to stay neutral."

"And the Gaza situation? When does that reach a tipping point?"

"October 2025 is key. Many recent psychic visions of our team describe a "forced resolution" around this time. With Saturn in Pisces pressuring humanitarian crises, I foresee a U.S.-brokered deal to relocate Gazans to Jordan and Egypt, finalized by late October. This won't be peaceful—it'll follow a summer of stalled ceasefires and a major Israel operation in Rafah to root out Hamas remnants."

"What about Iran's role beyond the nuclear threat?"

"Early 2026 is when Iran becomes the wildcard. Psychic narratives mention "a leader's health failing" coinciding with Jupiter's retrograde in Gemini. Power struggles in Tehran could spill into proxy wars, with Iraq's Shiite militias launching attacks on U.S. bases in Syria by February 2026. This aligns with the astrological "Mars-Saturn square" in January 2026—a classic war aspect."

"Any hope for de-escalation by mid-2026?"

"June 2026 brings a potential pivot. Neptune's retrograde in Aries softens ideological rigidity, and there's consensus among seers that Saudi Arabia will step in as a mediator. If Iran's internal chaos stabilizes, we might see a regional summit focused on rebuilding Gaza and containing Hezbollah. But it'll be fragile—Venus conjunct Pluto in Capricorn that month hints at backroom deals and hidden agendas."

"So the timeline's clear: March '25 lights the fuse, late summer explodes, and '26 is either cleanup or chaos."

"Exactly. And remember—these dates aren't set in stone. Free will and diplomacy can shift outcomes, but the planetary and psychic patterns suggest a narrow window for intervention. The Middle East in 2025-26 is a pressure cooker; it's not if it vents, but when and how."

I was ready to move on.

"Lisa, we've talked about Ukraine and the Middle East, but what about India and Pakistan? There's been so much tension lately—are things really as dangerous as they seem? What do you see happening?"

Lisa replied, slightly relieved that we were moving on. "You're right, the situation between India and Pakistan is extremely volatile right now, and the astrological and psychic predictions are pretty clear that we're entering a "dangerous period" for the whole region—India, Pakistan, and even Bangladesh. From May 18 through June 7, 2025, Mars is debilitated and Rahu (the North Node) changes signs. This is a classic recipe for heightened military risk, accidents, and political instability. It's a time when tempers flare, mistakes happen, and there's a real possibility of further escalation—especially with both sides on edge after the recent strikes and retaliations."

"Does that mean we're looking at a full-scale war? Or is there a chance things calm down after June?"

"The predictions suggest that while the risk is very real through June, the conflict doesn't explode into a nuclear war. In fact, almost every major source says nuclear weapons won't be used in 2025 or 2026, even if the threats are made. What's more likely is a multi-front conflict: Pakistan isn't just dealing with India, but also internal fragmentation. There are strong signs of separatist movements gaining ground in Balochistan and two more provinces plus Taliban pressure from Afghanistan. The fragmentation could be even more dramatic, starting late 2025 and continuing into 2026."

"That's intense. What about August, September, and October? Are there more flashpoints ahead?"

"Absolutely. August through October 2025 is flagged as another highly sensitive window. September and October, in particular, are marked by astrologers and psychics as months with potential for major incidents—airstrikes, political crises, even the risk of a plane crash. India is expected to act with restraint, but if provoked, there could be significant advances into a disputed region. Full integration of these territories is seen as a multi-year process, but the groundwork could be laid this fall. Meanwhile, Pakistan's own political system is predicted to collapse around late May, accelerating internal chaos and civil unrest."

I wanted to understand the extent of the conflicts. "Does China get involved? And what happens to ordinary people in both countries?"

"China is expected to provide covert support to Pakistan but not intervene directly—at least for now. Interestingly, China itself is predicted to face internal instability by 2027, so its focus may shift inward. For people on the ground, the risks are real: major Indian cities like Delhi and Mumbai could face missile threats, though India's defenses are expected to hold. Both countries will see economic volatility, possible civil unrest, and a need for resilience—especially around food security and disaster preparedness. The conflict is expected to drag on at least into late 2026, with sporadic violence and instability continuing even longer. Fragmentation of Pakistan and broader regional realignment are the most likely outcomes, but the good news is that, despite the scale of the crisis, there's no sign of a global or nuclear war on the horizon."

"So, it's a long, rough road ahead, but not the end of the world."

"Exactly. The next year and a half will be a crucible for the region, but it's more about transformation than total destruction. The hope is that, out of all this turmoil, new structures and alliances will emerge—and that, in time, the region can move toward greater stability and even healing."

"So eventually everyone heals?"

"That is the strength of the human heart. It heals wounds. Hopefully it learns as well but history has a strange way of repeating itself. Sometime the repetition take a long time but it happens."

OUR CONVERSATION WENT back to Israel - Iran and the Middle East later in the conversation so posting these details here.

We sat in Lisa's living room, the late afternoon sun slanting through the window, notebooks and tea at hand. The air was heavy with the sense that the Middle East was once again on the brink. I leaned forward, voice low.

"So, Lisa, let's talk again about the big one—Israel and Iran. There is a lot of concern here. There's so much tension, so many rumors. What do you see for the future of this conflict?"

Lisa's eyes darkened, her tone measured. "The psychic and astrological patterns for 2025 are clear: the Israel-Iran confrontation is the most dangerous flashpoint of the year. The risk of a direct military clash is higher than it's been in decades, and it doesn't just threaten those two countries—it could redraw the map of the entire region." She paused, flipping through her notes. "Let's break it down."

The Build-Up: Early to Mid-2025

Lisa continued, "The year starts with a sense of mounting pressure. Iran's nuclear program is front and center—there are consistent predictions that Iran either has, or is very close to having, enough enriched uranium for multiple nuclear weapons. This sets off alarm bells in Israel and among its Western allies. The psychic visions and astrological charts both point to March 2025 as a critical turning point: a rare six-planet conjunction in Pisces, plus a solar eclipse, creates the kind of cosmic turbulence that often coincides with dramatic geopolitical moves."

I scribbled notes. "So, March is when the fuse is lit?"

She nodded. "Exactly. There's a sense of frantic diplomatic activity, back-channel warnings, and last-ditch efforts to avoid war. But the consensus is that these efforts stall—neither side is willing to back down. Iran ramps up its rhetoric and military exercises; Israel moves forces and signals it's ready to act."

The Strike: Summer 2025

Lisa's voice grew tense. "Late June through September is the danger zone. Multiple independent sources—psychics, astrologers, even military analysts—see a 'sudden and unexpected' military event in this window. The most consistent vision is of Israel launching a major airstrike on Iran's nuclear facilities, using advanced bunker-busting bombs. The strike is calculated, not impulsive—timed to maximize surprise and minimize Iranian retaliation, but it's still a massive gamble."

I felt a chill. "What happens next?"

She leaned in. "Immediate regional fallout. Iran retaliates, but not with a full-scale invasion. Instead, the conflict spreads through proxies:

Hezbollah launches rocket barrages from Lebanon, Houthi drones target Red Sea shipping, and Iranian-backed militias in Iraq and Syria strike U.S. and Israeli interests. There's even a vision of a major submarine incident in the Middle East—possibly a nuclear-powered vessel suffering a fire or explosion near a major city, with a Western aircraft carrier nearby. The details are murky, but it's clear that the naval theater becomes a new front in the conflict."

Escalation and Global Impact

Lisa's tone was grave. "The psychic consensus is that this isn't World War III—but it's the closest the world has come in a generation. Oil prices spike, global markets shudder, and there's a real risk of cyberattacks targeting Western infrastructure. Iran experiences a planned communications blackout, with government officials going underground. There's also a prediction of toxic chemical or radiation release in Iran, possibly from the strikes on underground facilities, creating a humanitarian crisis in desert regions."

I pressed, "Does the U.S. get pulled in directly?"

She shook her head. "The U.S. tries to stay one step removed, but it's drawn in by necessity. There are visions of U.S. naval forces intervening to stabilize shipping lanes and help key allies. Proxy wars heat up, and the risk of accidental escalation is high. But the psychic threads are clear: no nuclear weapons are used, and the confrontation, while severe, remains contained to the region."

Turning Point: Late 2025 to Early 2026

I asked, "How does it end? Or does it?"

Lisa's answer was cautious. "By October 2025, there's a forced resolution. The psychic visions describe a U.S.-brokered deal that involves major concessions—possibly Israel agreeing to limited strikes in exchange for international monitoring of Iran's program, and Iran pulling back its proxies under pressure from Russia and China. There's also mention of internal turmoil in Iran: the Ayatollah faces a health crisis, and civil unrest grows, especially after a high-profile female spy case triggers protests."

She added, "Early 2026 is when the energy shifts. Iran's leadership is in flux—power struggles erupt, and Shiite militias in Iraq become more aggressive. But the worst of the Israel-Iran confrontation is over. Saudi Arabia steps in as a mediator, and a fragile regional summit is convened to address reconstruction and de-escalation. The peace is uneasy, but the risk of all-out war recedes."

The Long View: 2026 and Beyond

I exhaled, letting the tension out. "So, what's the legacy of this war?"

Lisa smiled, bittersweet. "The psychic and astrological consensus is that the 2025 Israel-Iran war is a crucible—a test that forces the region to confront old patterns of violence and retaliation. The aftermath is messy: mass migration, economic hardship, and a humanitarian crisis in parts of Iran and Gaza. But by 2027, there's a slow shift toward rebuilding. Saudi Arabia and the UAE take a bigger role in reconstruction, and grassroots peace efforts gain traction. The old order is shaken, and while the scars are deep, the seeds of a new, more pragmatic regional balance are planted."

She finished, "It's not the apocalypse. It's a painful, necessary reckoning—one that could, if leaders are wise, mark the beginning of the end for endless Middle Eastern wars."

We sat in silence, the weight of the future hanging between us, but also a glimmer of hope that even the darkest cycles can, eventually, be broken.

United States

As we stepped out of Lisa's cozy cottage and onto a winding trail, she grinned and handed me a walking stick. "Come on," she said, "let's take this conversation to the mountains. The fresh air always helps clear the psychic cobwebs."

The path wound through the foothills of the Rockies, sunlight flickering through the pines, the air crisp and full of possibility. Lisa walked ahead, boots crunching on gravel, her scarf trailing behind her like a flag of curiosity. "You know," she said, glancing back, "after ten years of working together on these books, I think the mountains are the only place where we haven't tried to predict the future yet. Remember that time in Sedona when I was interviewing that psychic and, out of nowhere, I started finishing her sentences? I thought she was going to fall off her meditation cushion in shock. I'm still not sure if I was channeling her or just picking up her lunch order."

I laughed, remembering the look of mutual amazement—and a little dismay—on both their faces. "You've always had a knack for getting in the zone, Lisa. You're psychic yourself, so that's expected."

She shrugged, smiling. "Maybe it's just all the years of soaking up cosmic energy, first with the family, then my mentors and maybe some with you. Or maybe it's what happens when you spend a decade knee-deep in prophecies, spreadsheets, and the occasional incense cloud. Either way, the universe has a sense of humor—and so do we. Now, let's see what the stars and the world's psychics have in store for humanity's next chapter. And if I start predicting your coffee order, you'll know I have gone too far."

As we made our way up the sun-dappled trail, Lisa grinned and nudged me with her elbow. "You know, people always think interviewing psychics is all incense and deep wisdom, but sometimes it's just plain weird—and hilarious." She paused, catching her breath. "Like that time in Santa Fe, when I was interviewing that famous trance medium. I was so tuned in that I started answering her questions before she even asked them. She just stared at me, wide-eyed, and said, 'Wait, are you reading my mind now?' For a second, I thought I'd accidentally swapped jobs!"

I laughed, and Lisa shook her head, clearly amused by the memory. "And then there was that psychic fair in Boulder. I was interviewing this guy who claimed he could channel the wisdom of ancient Atlanteans. Halfway through, his crystal ball rolled off the table, landed on my foot, and he said, 'That's a sign your energy is too strong for this room.' I told him it was more likely a sign he needed a better table. He didn't think it was funny, but the rest of the psychics did. Honestly, after a decade of this, I have learned: always expect the unexpected, and never underestimate the universe's sense of humor—or its ability to keep us humble."

"Let's continue our conversation. How is US going to be doing?"

As we reached a scenic overlook, Lisa paused to catch her breath and gaze out over the endless sweep of the Rockies. "You know," she said, "if you want to talk about a country in transition, the U.S. in 2025 is the poster child. All the big astrological alignments—especially that rare six-planet conjunction in Pisces on March 29—are pointing to a year of major turbulence and transformation. It's like a cosmic reset button is being pressed, and nothing's off-limits: government, the economy, even the collective mood of the nation is up for review."

I nodded, watching a hawk circle far below. "So, it's not just political drama or economic ups and downs—it's something deeper?"

"Exactly," Lisa replied. "It's a year of upheaval, but also of awakening. Both the psychics and the Vedic astrologers keep calling 2025 a turning point for collective consciousness. There's a sense that, even though it's going to be a bumpy ride, this is the start of a new era—one where the U.S. leads a global shift toward greater truth, compassion, and innovation. It's not without pain, but it's the kind of pain that comes before real renewal. Think of it as a necessary crucible, burning away what's outdated so something better can take root."

She grinned, nudging me with her elbow. "So, while the headlines might scream chaos, if you look beneath the surface, you'll see the seeds of something much bigger—a spiritual and social awakening that could define the next chapter not just for America, but for the whole world."

As we followed a winding trail through the pines, Lisa glanced over with a mischievous glint. "You ready for some political fortune-telling, Rocky Mountain style? Because the U.S. in 2025 is about to get wilder than a Colorado thunderstorm."

I laughed. "With Trump back in the White House, I'm guessing we're in for more than just a few political lightning bolts?"

Lisa nodded, picking her way over a root. "You could say that. The predictions are clear: the Trump presidency kicks off with fireworks—legal battles, constitutional drama, and enough protests to keep every sign-maker in business. There's even talk of more threats. It's high-stakes, high-drama, and the country's mood swings more than a pendulum in a hurricane."

I raised an eyebrow. "And what about all this 'end of woke' talk? Is that real or just political theater?"

"Oh, it's real—at least in the sense that Trump's team is expected to push a wave of anti-woke laws," Lisa replied, grinning. "Think restrictions on gender education, bathroom policies, and more. Cue the backlash: protests, legal fights, even riots in some cities. It's like Congress and the country are locked in a never-ending tug-of-war, and nobody's letting go of the rope. The polarization isn't just in D.C.—it's in the streets, the courts, and Thanksgiving dinner conversations."

I shook my head, half amused, half exasperated. "And the scandals? There's always a scandal."

Lisa chuckled. "Oh, you bet. The Epstein files are predicted to drop bombshells—politicians, Hollywood, even judges could get caught in the fallout. Public trust in institutions? Let's just say it's not trending upward. Plus, new claims of voter fraud might lead to a referendum or even a legal battle over whether Trump could go for a third term. The Constitution's about to get more attention than it's had in decades."

I glanced at the mountain vista, trying to imagine the world stage. "So, does all this drama change America's place in the world?"

Lisa stopped, taking in the view. "Absolutely. Trump's 'America First' is back—pulling troops from Europe, expanding bases in the UK and the Pacific, and cutting big trade deals, especially with the UK. There's even a rumor about a Disney theme park on the Isle of Wight—because why not? He'll push Taiwan to move manufacturing to the U.S. for protection from China, and there's talk of a new Western alliance: U.S., UK, Canada, Australia and a few countries all banding together to counter China. It's a whole new geopolitical chessboard, with Trump playing to win."

She grinned at me, sunlight flickering through the trees. "So, if you thought American politics was dramatic before, just wait. There is a public disagreement between Vance and Macron that for some reason, has come in many visions. The next act is about to begin—and the universe, apparently, has front-row seats."

As we followed a narrow trail, the pine needles crunching underfoot, Lisa glanced over with a grin. "You know, if you want to get a real sense of what's in store for the U.S. in 2025 and 2026, you have to look at the numbers as well as the stars. Numerology has a lot to say about this cycle—especially when it comes to politics."

I laughed. "All right, Lisa, hit me with the numbers. What's the vibe for the U.S. in 2025 and 2026?"

She nodded, thoughtful. "2025 is an 9 year for the United States when you add up the digits—2+0+2+5 equals 9. In numerology, 9 is the number of endings, reckoning, and transformation. It's a year when old cycles complete and the country is forced to confront what's no longer working. Think of it as a national 'cleaning house'—politically, socially, and even spiritually. It's no surprise that the predictions talk about major legal battles, constitutional drama, and a wave of anti-woke laws. There's this sense of things reaching a boiling point, with the possibility of big revelations, scandals, and a lot of public reckoning."

I raised an eyebrow. "So, 2025 is about closing chapters. What about 2026?"

Lisa smiled, picking her way over a mossy rock. "2026 is a 1 year—2+0+2+6 equals 10, and 1+0 makes 1. That's the number of new beginnings, leadership, and fresh starts. So after all the drama, protests, and polarization of 2025, 2026 is about forging a new path. It's a time when new leaders can emerge, new policies take root, and the country starts to rebuild from the ashes of whatever burned down the year before. It's not all smooth sailing—there's still plenty of tension, especially with the big planetary alignments—but the energy shifts from endings to beginnings."

I grinned. "So, if 2025 is the year the U.S. finally cleans out the political attic, 2026 is when it starts remodeling?"

Lisa laughed. "Exactly! And with all the astrological action—Saturn moving into Pisces, Jupiter's big shifts, and all those eclipses—it's like the universe is handing the U.S. a broom in one hand and a blueprint in the other. The next two years are a wild ride, but if the country can survive the shakeup, it's got a real shot at a new chapter. Just don't expect it to be boring—numerology promises a plot twist or two before the credits roll."

We'd barely rounded the next bend in the trail when Lisa stopped, squinting up at a sky that was already hinting at summer thunderheads. "You want to talk about predictions that hit close to home?" she said, waving her hand at the horizon. "Let's talk weather. Because if these predictions are right, 2025 is going to be a wild ride for the U.S.—and not just politically."

I grinned, pulling my jacket a little tighter. "So what's in store? More of the usual, or are we talking next-level drama?"

Lisa chuckled. "Let's just say, keep your rain boots, fire extinguisher, and emergency snacks handy. The consensus is that we'll see extremes on both coasts. The West—especially California and the Pacific Northwest—faces a serious fire season, with predictions of major blazes and smoky skies from June through September. Some sources even mention the possibility of a significant earthquake, especially around New York, with late summer months flagged as sensitive periods."

She paused to let that sink in before continuing. "Meanwhile, the East Coast and Midwest are in for a different kind of drama: flooding. There are repeated warnings about excessive rainfall, swollen rivers, and flash floods—especially from late spring into early fall. Places that are usually dry could see sudden, intense storms. And with the six-planet conjunction in Pisces in late March, astrologers say the oceans themselves are restless, raising concerns about hurricanes and even tsunamis in the Atlantic and Gulf regions."

I raised an eyebrow. "Sounds like Mother Nature is in a mood. Anything about tornadoes or other surprises?"

Lisa nodded. "Definitely. The planetary alignments—especially Saturn's move into Pisces and Mars' tense aspects in June and July—suggest a spike in tornadoes and severe storms across the central states. There's also talk of a 'fire and water cleansing'—meaning not just wildfires and floods, but the kind of weather that disrupts crops and power grids. A prediction in our last meeting even warns of unexplained fires and agricultural collapse, which could hit food supplies and prices hard."

She looked at me, serious for a moment. "And let's not forget the health angle. The combination of heatwaves, humidity, and flooding brings a higher risk of weather-related illnesses and even the spread of new pathogens—something psychics have flagged. The advice? Stay prepared, stay flexible, and don't take blue skies for granted. 2025 isn't a year to ignore the forecast—or the wisdom of a well-stocked pantry."

Lisa smiled, her tone lightening again as we walked on. "But hey, if all else fails, maybe this is the year we finally get that emergency weather radio we've been talking about. Or, you know, just move our meetings to a nice, climate-controlled coffee shop. Either way, the universe is making sure we don't get bored."

As we made our way along the ridge, Lisa paused and looked out over the valley. "If you want specifics, this year's weather is one for the record books—and not in a way that'll make the travel brochures," she said, half-smiling.

"Let's start with June," she continued. "The astrological charts and psychic predictions agree: the West, especially California and the Pacific Northwest, is staring down another intense fire season. The risk starts ramping up in late June and peaks in July and August, with the worst fires likely in northern California, Oregon, and possibly even into Idaho. A vision we had mentions 'major fires in the West'—and some astrologers point to Mars-Saturn tension in early July as a trigger for rapid wildfire spread."

I winced. "And the East Coast? Are we in for another hurricane parade?"

Lisa nodded. "Absolutely. The East Coast and Gulf states are in the cross-hairs for hurricanes and flooding, especially from late August through October. The six-planet conjunction in Pisces back in March is still sending ripples, and the charts show heightened oceanic activity. Florida, the Carolina, and even up to New York could see severe storms and flooding. There's even a psychic prediction of a 'major earthquake in New York'—with September or October flagged as sensitive months for seismic or storm-related disruption."

She paused to catch her breath as we climbed a steeper section. "And don't forget the Midwest. Between June and September, tornadoes and violent storms are likely to spike, especially across Oklahoma, Kansas, Missouri, and Illinois. The Mars transit in Leo and the nodal shift in May are classic signals for extreme weather in the heartland. There's also talk of flash floods in places that are usually dry—Nebraska, Iowa, even parts of Texas. July and August are especially dicey."

I glanced up at the sky, half-expecting it to answer. "Any curveballs for the rest of the country?"

Lisa grinned. "Wouldn't be 2025 without a few surprises. Visions and predictions warn about 'unexplained fires' and agricultural collapse in the Southeast, especially Georgia and Alabama, late summer into early fall. There's also a risk of a major dam breach or flooding event in the Rockies or upper Midwest—late July is the window to watch. And, just to keep us on our toes, some psychics mention a 'tower block fire' in a major U.S. city, though they're cagey about which one."

She finished with a sigh and a smile. "So, in short: June brings fire risk to the West, July and August crank up the heat and storms across the Midwest, August to October is hurricane and flood season for the East and Gulf, and the South and Rockies get their own wild cards. If you've got travel plans, keep your weather app—and maybe your emergency kit—close."

"I won't have expected anything else", I said. "Based on how this year started."

As we stepped over a patch of wildflowers, I glanced at Lisa. "So, with all this cosmic chaos, what do the stars and psychics say about inflation in the U.S. this year? My grocery bills have already started acting like they're on a roller coaster."

Lisa laughed. "You're not imagining it. The consensus—astrologers and psychics—is that 2025 is a year of economic turbulence, and inflation is right at the heart of it. The big planetary shifts—Saturn's entry into Pisces in March, Jupiter's move into Gemini in May—are classic signals for financial volatility. The psychic predictions echo this: expect sharp price swings, supply chain hiccups, and a lot of nervous energy in the markets, especially from June onward."

She paused, scanning the horizon as if she could see the numbers rising in the clouds. "The months to watch are June through October. Astrologers point to the Mars-Saturn dynamic in June and July as a trigger for sudden spikes in prices—especially food, fuel, and essentials. There's talk of shortages or at least the perception of them, which only adds to the inflationary pressure. July and August are flagged for market corrections and possible panic buying, particularly around holidays and back-to-school season."

I sighed. "So, it's not just my imagination that everything's getting more expensive?"

Lisa shook her head. "Not at all. The predictions say inflation will hit hardest in the summer, then start to ease a bit by late fall—but don't expect prices to drop back to 2023 levels. The U.S. will see some stabilization by early 2026, but the new normal is higher costs for food, housing, and energy. The advice from both the stars and the sages? Avoid risky investments after mid-May, don't get greedy, and keep a close eye on your budget. There's also a warning about cyber attacks and digital disruptions—so even things like online banking and payments could get bumpy."

She grinned, nudging me playfully. "On the bright side, the same cosmic shake-up that brings inflation also brings opportunity. Jupiter in Gemini is great for innovation and new business ideas, especially in tech and communication. If you can ride out the storm, there's a chance to come out ahead. Just don't expect the universe—or your wallet—to make it easy."

We walked on, the wind picking up as if to underscore her point. "So, in short," Lisa said, "Inflation is real, but so is the potential for personal growth and adaptation. And hey, if all else fails, maybe it's time to start that backyard vegetable garden we've been joking about. At least then we'll have tomatoes, even if the world goes sideways."

I shook my head, chuckling. "Honestly, Lisa, with the way inflation and shrinkflation are going, I'm starting to think my next box of cereal will just come with a magnifying glass and a note that says, 'Contents may have settled during shipping—and also during the last economic cycle.'"

Lisa and I found a sunny spot to rest, and I couldn't resist steering the conversation toward the economy—my favorite mix of anxiety and hope. "So, Lisa, after all these weather and inflation predictions, what do the stars and psychics say about the U.S. economy and the stock market for the rest of 2025 and into 2026?"

Lisa grinned, pulling out her notebook. "Well, get ready for a bumpy ride. The consensus from astrologers and psychics is that 2025 is a year of serious economic turbulence, especially starting in June. The big planetary shifts—Saturn's entry into Pisces in late March, Jupiter's move into Gemini in mid-May, and the Mars-Saturn dynamic in June and July—are all classic signals for market volatility and financial shakeups."

She flipped a page and continued, "The months to watch are May through October. Astrologers flag May 13 as the start of stock market volatility, with Jupiter's sign change on May 14 adding to the tension. There's a warning about rapid corrections and sudden drops, especially in June and July, when Mars and Saturn are in a tense aspect. The advice is clear: avoid risky investments after mid-May and don't get greedy. Even some prophecies warn of a 'major economic crisis' and market upheavals, with the potential for repeated shocks through the summer and into early fall."

I leaned in, curious. "So, is this just another roller coaster, or are we talking about a real crash?"

Lisa nodded, thoughtful. "It's more than just a few dips. The predictions suggest a 'rocky year' for global finance, with the U.S. experiencing sharp swings—especially in stocks, real estate, and even cryptocurrency. There's talk of shortages and supply chain issues, particularly around the holidays—think Thanksgiving and Christmas—so prices could spike and certain goods might become hard to find. The psychic consensus is that while there's no total collapse, there will be enough volatility to make even seasoned investors nervous."

She added, "On the flip side, there's also opportunity. Jupiter in Gemini is great for innovation, tech, and communications, so sectors tied to AI, automation, and smart infrastructure might actually thrive amid the chaos. There's mention of tech leaders playing a big role, with some tension between Musk and Trump over government contracts. But the overall advice? Stay nimble, diversify, and don't expect the old rules to apply."

Lisa looked out at the distant mountains, her tone softening. "By early 2026, things start to stabilize a bit. The wild swings ease up, and the economy finds a new normal—though it's not the same as before. The stars suggest this is a reset, not a return to the past. So, if you can ride out the storm and keep your head, there's a good chance you'll come out stronger on the other side. Just don't expect a smooth journey—2025 is all about transformation, and the markets are along for the ride."

Lisa and I found a shady boulder to rest on, and I couldn't help but nudge the conversation toward the stock market. "Okay, Lisa, let's get real—when do the stars and psychics say we should brace for the next market roller coaster? I'd like to know when to hide my phone from my brokerage app."

Lisa grinned. "You and half of Wall Street! The cosmic consensus is clear: 2025 is a year of volatility, and the calendar is practically sprinkled with 'handle with care' stickers. Let's break it down month by month, because some of these dates are... well, let's just say, not for the faint of heart."

She flipped through her notes. "First up, May is the opening act. The advice is to avoid big investments after May 13—unless you enjoy living dangerously."

I raised an eyebrow. "So, May is the appetizer. What about the main course?"

Lisa laughed. "June and July are where things get spicy. Mars and Saturn are in a tense aspect from June 7 through late July, and that's classic astrology for market shocks, sudden drops, and wild swings. Some psychics even call this the 'summer of surprises'—not the fun kind, unless you enjoy financial whiplash. Many psychics warn of 'alarming periods' in late June. So if you see your favorite stock doing the cha-cha, don't say the universe didn't warn you."

She leaned in, lowering her voice for dramatic effect. "August and September? Not much calmer. The Rahu-Ketu nodal shift in May sets the stage for 82 days of financial turbulence, peaking in August and September. Astrologers say this is when the 'fake economy' gets exposed—so expect corrections, maybe even a sudden drop or two. If you're still holding on for dear life by October, give yourself a gold star."

I couldn't help but snort. "So basically, the only thing more volatile than the market is my mood if I check my portfolio too often?"

Lisa grinned. "Exactly! And don't forget the holidays—there's a warning about shortages and price spikes around Thanksgiving and Christmas. So if you're planning to buy gifts, maybe start early... or just give everyone a hug and a homemade coupon for 'one free market pep talk.' The cosmic advice? Stay nimble, diversify, and don't let the headlines—or your brokerage app—ruin your summer."

She winked. "And if you see me buying extra coffee in June, you'll know I'm preparing for the next round of cosmic chaos. At least caffeine is still a safe investment—so far!"

Lisa took a sip of her water and grinned as I asked about the "wild world of alternative investments." "Oh, you mean the emotional roller coaster that is crypto, gold, and silver? Grab your seatbelt—2025 is not for the faint of heart," she said, waving her notebook like a game show host about to reveal the next big prize.

She started with crypto, her tone half-serious, half-amused. "All the big psychic and astrological sources see 2025 as a year where cryptocurrency, especially Bitcoin, stays strong and even gains legitimacy. Trump's administration is predicted to be quietly supportive, so don't be surprised if you see less regulatory drama and more mainstream adoption. But—and this is a big but—expect wild swings. The months around June, and again in September are especially volatile. If you're the type who checks prices every hour, maybe invest in a stress ball too."

I raised an eyebrow. "So, crypto is still the wild west, but with a few more sheriffs in town?"

Lisa laughed. "Exactly. And don't forget, they warn about cyber attacks and digital disruptions, especially in July and October. So, back up your wallets, double-check your passwords, and maybe don't keep your life savings in a meme coin."

She turned the page, her eyes twinkling. "Now, gold and silver—this is where the old-school investors get to feel smug. The predictions are clear: with all the market volatility, inflation, and geopolitical drama, precious metals are in for a strong year. Gold, in particular, is flagged to spike during periods of stock market turbulence—especially in June, July, and again in September. Silver follows suit, but with even wilder swings. If you're looking for a safe haven, gold is your friend. If you're looking for a thrill ride, silver's your ticket."

I couldn't help but joke, "So, should I bury some gold in the backyard, or just buy a metal detector and start digging up the neighbor's lawn?"

Lisa grinned. "Honestly, with the way 2025 is shaping up, maybe both! Metals are likely to outperform most traditional assets during the rough patches, especially when the market gets jittery over inflation or global conflict. But remember, the same cosmic forces that boost gold can also trigger sudden corrections—so don't put all your eggs, or gold bars, in one basket."

She finished with a wink. "And if you're feeling really adventurous, keep an eye on rare earth metals and new tech-related commodities. Jupiter in Gemini is all about innovation, so anything tied to electronics, batteries, or AI could see surprise gains—just expect a few plot twists along the way. In short: 2025 is the year to diversify, stay nimble, and maybe keep a little gold coin in your pocket for luck. At the very least, it'll make for a great conversation starter at the next neighborhood barbecue."

I asked, "What happens to tech stock?", noting the stocks that I see in the news daily.

Lisa stretched her legs and gave me a sly grin. "So, you want to know about tech stocks in 2025? Well, let's just say the stars, the sages, and even the psychics all agree: buckle up, because it's going to be a Silicon Valley soap opera."

She flipped open her notebook, pages bristling with cosmic scribbles. "First, the big picture: 2025 is a year of wild swings for tech. Jupiter's move into Gemini in mid-May is like pouring rocket fuel on innovation—AI, automation, communications, and anything 'smart' are in the cosmic spotlight. But—and this is a big but—Jupiter's journey is anything but smooth. There's a lot of volatility, especially June through September, thanks to that Mars-Saturn tension and the infamous Rahu-Ketu nodal shift. So, if you're a tech investor, maybe keep your seatbelt—and your antacids—handy."

I chuckled. "So, we're talking moonshots and meteoric drops, all in the same quarter?"

Lisa nodded. "Exactly. The predictions say we could see tech stocks soar on big news—think AI breakthroughs, new smart city projects, or even quantum leaps in computing. Elon Musk, as usual, is in the thick of it: SpaceX and Tesla are flagged for major headlines, and there's even a psychic prediction of Musk butting heads with Trump over government contracts. But every cosmic high comes with a correction. June and July are especially dicey—market shocks, sudden drops, and a few 'what just happened?' moments. If you're planning to brag about your portfolio, maybe wait until October."

She grinned, "And don't forget the cyber side. Our visions warn about cyber attacks and digital disruptions, especially in July and October. So, if your favorite tech stock tanks because of a ransomware headline, don't say the universe didn't warn you. On the flip side, cybersecurity firms could see a windfall—2025 might be the year 'digital defense' becomes the new buzzword on Wall Street."

I raised an eyebrow. "So, is it all doom and gloom, or are there bright spots?"

Lisa laughed. "There are definite bright spots! Jupiter in Gemini is great for companies that pivot fast and innovate—AI, cloud, green tech, and anything that helps people work smarter, not harder. But the cosmic advice is clear: don't chase hype, and don't get greedy. The market's going to reward brains and adaptability, not just big promises. And if you're tempted to buy the dip in June or July, maybe check your horoscope first—or at least your caffeine supply."

She closed her notebook with a flourish. "So, in summary: 2025 is a blockbuster year for tech, but it's more 'edge-of-your-seat thriller' than 'feel-good drama.' Play smart, stay nimble, and remember—sometimes the best investment is a little cosmic humor."

As we rounded a bend in the trail, I turned to Lisa, lowering my voice as if the pines themselves might be listening. "Lisa, with everything going on, what do the stars and psychics say about terrorism and public unrest this year? Are we in for more shocks, or is there a chance things calm down?"

Lisa took a deep breath, her expression turning serious. "Honestly? The consensus from the psychics, astrologers, and even channeled predictions is that 2025 is a year of heightened tension—especially from June through the fall. The planetary alignments are classic for unrest: Mars and Saturn are at odds from early June through late July, which is a textbook setup for conflict, agitation, and, unfortunately, the risk of terror attacks or public violence. The U.S. isn't immune, but the focus is especially sharp in South Asia, the Middle East, and parts of Europe."

She flipped through her notes, frowning slightly. "For the U.S., the predictions point to a spike in public unrest around the times of major political or legal developments—think June and July, when Mars is especially active, and again in September and October, when the nodes shift and the market jitters add fuel to the fire. There's a real risk of protests turning violent, especially in big cities. Some psychics even mention the possibility of a 'tower block deserted'—which could mean an evacuation due to a threat or attack, though they're vague about the details."

I hesitated, then asked, "What about terrorism specifically? Are there any regions or months we need to be extra cautious about?"

Lisa nodded. "Yes, unfortunately. The summer months—June through September—are flagged as periods of higher risk, both for domestic unrest and for targeted attacks. The predictions warn about 'internal strikes' and counter terrorism operations, particularly in regions already on edge. For the U.S., the risk is highest around July 4th and again in late September, when political polarization and economic anxiety hit a peak. There's also a warning about cyber-attacks and digital disruptions—so even if it's not physical violence, we could see chaos in the form of infrastructure or communication failures."

She gave a wry smile. "On the plus side, the predictions don't see these events spiraling into full-scale war or total collapse. The idea is more of a series of shocks—unsettling, yes, but ultimately survivable. The advice is to stay alert, avoid crowds during tense periods, and keep your digital life as secure as your front door."

Lisa looked up to the sky, looking thoughtful as I asked, "There are so many rumors about leaders facing health scares or assassination attempts. What do the predictions say about Donald Trump specifically?"

She nodded, "That's a question a lot of people are asking—and the predictions are surprisingly detailed. Multiple psychic and astrological sources foresee a health scare or internal threat. The good news? He survives. It's dramatic, but not fatal, and it becomes a major headline—another chapter in the saga."

I leaned in, "What about his health? There's been a lot of speculation."

Lisa replied, "There are also warnings about Trump's health, particularly his physical and mental stamina. Some psychics see him facing a significant health issue—possibly requiring surgery or even time in a wheelchair—especially as we move into the second half of 2025 and into September. During these periods, it's predicted that his vice president, JD Vance, could temporarily take over presidential duties during Trump's recovery."

I raised an eyebrow, "Does this mean he steps down or loses power?"

Lisa shook her head. "No, the consensus is that while these health scares and other rumors are serious, Trump remains in office. There's no prediction of him stepping down or being removed. In fact, the legal and political drama around him only intensifies, with ongoing constitutional battles and public debate. But through it all, he's still at the center of U.S. politics—surviving, adapting, and, as always, making headlines."

Lisa leaned forward, her face etched with the gravity of the moment. "You know, this summer and fall, it's as if the world's stage is set for a reckoning among leaders everywhere—not just Trump. The astrological alignments and psychic patterns for 2025 are strikingly clear: nearly every major head of state faces a personal or political crisis, and some will not make it through the year unchanged."

She started with Trump, her tone measured but urgent. "For Trump, the warnings are focused on potential health issues. Any leader always has security concerns and no leader of a major country is immune from such a threat. While I hope things don't change, there is a possibility that the mood in the U.S. shifts overnight: a collective exhale, a sense of karmic closure, and the beginning of a new chapter as power transitions to his successor."

Lisa paused, then shifted to Iran. "But Trump isn't alone. Iran's Supreme Leader, the Ayatollah, is also in the crosshairs of fate. Predictions show a major health crisis—possibly while traveling—triggering internal chaos. There's a communications blackout, high-level officials going underground, and a dramatic female spy case that sparks civil unrest and mass protests. The leadership vacuum in Tehran could spill over into proxy wars, especially in Iraq and Syria, as rival factions vie for control."

She continued, "Putin's fate is equally precarious. The psychic consensus is that he faces a personal reckoning—either a dramatic health scare or a forced retreat from power. There's talk of scandals and internal betrayal, with his grip on Russia weakening as the Ukraine conflict grinds on. By late 2025 or early 2026, Putin may be sidelined, either by illness or by a palace coup. The Russian system is in flux, and new faces begin to emerge, though the transition is anything but smooth."

Lisa's voice softened as she mentioned Zelensky. "For Zelensky, the cards are turbulent. He's under immense pressure—scandals, corruption revelations, and a sense of being abandoned by allies. There's a strong possibility he resigns or is forced out within months, leaving under a cloud as Ukraine's political landscape fractures. The psychic threads suggest that his departure is not just personal, but symbolic—a sign that the old order in Kyiv is crumbling, making way for new, if uncertain, leadership."

She took a breath, then added, "And it's not just secular leaders. We already mentioned the change in the Pope in our 2025 Book of Predictions. There has been an attack on a Senator in US."

She took a breath, then added, "And don't overlook the UK. The predictions for the British premier are just as turbulent. Keir Starmer's government faces mounting economic chaos, with inflation, public sector strikes, and a housing crisis eroding confidence in Labor. There are strong signals that Starmer won't last the year as Prime Minister. Resignations are expected in his inner circle—including a Labor supporter with a history of substance abuse and a female MP stepping down over classified information leaks related to Gaza. The psychic consensus points to a possible coalition between the Conservatives and Nigel Farage's Reform Party, with Reform as the senior partner. The UK's political landscape is set for a major shake-up, and the turbulence won't stabilize until 2026."

Lisa looked out the window, her voice almost a whisper. "It's as if the universe has decided that 2025 is the year of the great turnover. Leaders fall, new ones rise, and nothing is guaranteed. The mood is anxious, volatile, but also full of possibility. The message is clear: no one is immune—not Trump, not the Ayatollah, not Putin, Zelensky, or even the Pope. The world is being forced to reckon with the limits of power, and the next few months will shape the course of history for years to come."

Financial Crisis

As we made our way back down the mountain trail, the late afternoon sun slanting through the pines, our boots crunching softly over gravel, the conversation turned reflective. The air was cooler now, the breeze carrying the scent of wild sage and pine needles. Lisa was quiet for a while, lost in thought as we navigated a narrow switchback.

I broke the silence. "Lisa, a lot of people are talking about a financial crisis and some kind of global reset. Is there really something big coming, or is it just the usual doomsday chatter?"

Lisa paused, looking out over the valley before answering. "It's not just chatter this time. The signals are everywhere—astrology, psychics, even the financial analysts are picking up on it. There's a consensus that we're heading for a major financial crisis in the next few years. But—" she hesitated, "—if you want specifics, 2025 and 2026 are the years to watch."

I cut in, "Let's focus on that. What do you see for 2025, month by month? When should we really buckle up?"

Lisa nodded, her tone shifting to business. "Alright, here's how it looks:"

"2025 starts with tension already in the air. The big astrological trigger is the six-planet conjunction, which is like a cosmic alarm clock for financial systems. But the real action begins in May. Around June mid, there seems to be a profound prediction for stock market volatility. That's when you'll want to keep an eye on your portfolio."

"So, May's the opening act. What about summer?"

"June and July are the main event. Astrologically, it's a combination that's historically linked to chaos, tech disruptions, and economic shocks. The consensus from psychics and astrologers is that June and July could see the 'biggest crash in world history'—not just in stocks, but also in crypto and banking. It's predicted to be sharp but short-lived, with recovery starting within a few weeks."

"And after that? Are we out of the woods?"

"Not quite. July 12 to October 7 is another danger zone, especially for banks. Astrologically—this is a classic setup for banking stress, possible failures of small and mid-sized banks, and even property market shocks. August and September could bring aftershocks, especially if there are cyber attacks or sudden global events."

Lisa smiled as we wandered beneath the tall pines, the quiet only broken by birdsong and the crunch of our boots. "You're right—it does feel almost surreal, doesn't it? Here we are, surrounded by all this peace, and yet the world out there is buzzing with talk of crisis and collapse. It's easy for those headlines to feel a million miles away."

She glanced at the sunlight dappling the trail. "That's the strange thing about big financial events—they always seem abstract until they land on your doorstep. But moments like this walk remind us to stay grounded, to appreciate what's real and present, even as we keep an eye on what's coming. The world might be unpredictable, but there's a lot to be said for finding calm in the chaos—even if it's just for a few hours out here."

I raised an eyebrow. "So, a crash, but not the end of the world?". I wanted some hope in this conversation.

"Exactly," Lisa said. "It's more like a cosmic wake-up call. The crash will hit stocks, crypto, and banking sectors hard. Small and mid-sized banks are particularly vulnerable from July through early October, when Saturn goes retrograde and Mars aspects Saturn. This could trigger failures and panic, but it's part of a larger financial reset—one that exposes the fragility of the current system and forces structural change."

I nodded slowly. "And after July? Is there a timeline for when things start to stabilize?"

Lisa smiled wryly. "Late summer and early fall remain tense, with aftershocks in August and September. But by October, the worst of the chaos should begin to settle. That's when governments might roll out debt restructuring plans and digital currency pilots. The reset isn't a single event; it's a process unfolding over months, with June and July as the dramatic opening act."

She glanced at me, eyes twinkling. "So, if you're thinking of investing, June and July are the months to be cautious—maybe hold tight, diversify, and keep a stash of patience. And maybe plant that garden we joked about earlier. It might be the safest investment of all."

I laughed, shaking my head. I'd always admired how Lisa could deliver even the grimmest forecasts with a glint of hope. "So, Lisa, how bad does it get with the banks? Are we talking just the U.S., or is this a global thing? Where do the dominos fall the hardest?"

Lisa smiled wryly. "It's not just the U.S.—though American small and mid-sized banks are especially at risk, according to both the astrologers and psychics. July through early October is the danger zone. We could see dozens, maybe even hundreds, of smaller banks fail or get absorbed. But Europe and parts of Asia aren't immune either. There's a ripple effect, especially in countries with shaky banking systems or heavy debt. India is flagged as another hotspot for bank failures, and even some EU nations could see trouble."

I frowned. "So, when the banks start wobbling, do governments actually step in? Or do they let the chips fall?"

Lisa nodded, her tone turning practical. "Governments will absolutely respond, but it's not a smooth process. Expect emergency meetings, new regulations, and a lot of political drama. In the U.S., the Fed and Treasury are likely to roll out backstops—think emergency lending and maybe even fast-tracked digital currency pilots. In Europe, you'll see coordinated bailouts, but there will be public anger over who gets rescued. India's government will also intervene, but it may be slower and less effective at first."

I raised an eyebrow. "And what about interest rates? Do they finally cut, or just keep talking about it?"

Lisa grinned. "That's the cosmic punchline! The predictions show central banks scrambling by late July and August. After months of stubborn rates, the crisis forces their hand. Expect sudden rate cuts—maybe even coordinated across the U.S., EU, and Asia. But it's a bit of a whiplash: rates drop fast to stabilize the system, but the relief is temporary. The bigger reset—debt restructuring, new rules, and digital currencies—comes later, as the dust settles into 2026."

She glanced at the trail ahead, sunlight flickering through the trees. "So, yes, it's a global shake-up. But if history—and the stars—are any guide, the world finds a way to patch things up, even if it means rewriting the rules along the way."

"What about property and real estate—residential and commercial? How big is the potential crash?"

Lisa nodded. "Real estate is in for a rough ride, too. The crash is expected to hit both residential and commercial sectors, especially in overheated markets. In the U.S., cities that saw the biggest pandemic booms—think Austin, Miami, Phoenix—are at risk for sharp corrections. Commercial real estate, especially office and retail, is the most vulnerable, with defaults and vacancies spiking from late summer into fall."

Lisa: "Globally, Europe's property markets—especially in Spain, Italy, and the UK—could also see steep drops, and India's overheated urban markets aren't immune. The banking crisis will spill over, with forced sales and tighter lending standards. Some predictions warn of price drops of 20-30% in the hardest-hit regions, with the pain peaking from August through October. Recovery will be slow, with prices stabilizing only as the broader economy finds its footing in 2026."

I laughed as the question popped into my head. "Okay, Lisa, if interest rates drop across the world, shouldn't that make it easier for buyers to jump into the property market? Or is there a catch?"

Lisa smiled, her eyes twinkling. "Great question! In theory, yes—lower rates should make mortgages more affordable and tempt buyers back in. But in reality, the picture's a lot messier this time. Even with rate cuts, banks will be much stricter about who they lend to, especially after all the shakeups and failures. Lending standards will tighten, and some banks just won't have the capacity or appetite to take on new risk."

I nodded, "So, even if the rates are low, not everyone will actually be able to get a loan?"

"Exactly," Lisa said. "Plus, with all the volatility and job losses, a lot of potential buyers are going to sit on the sidelines, worried about job security or falling prices. And for commercial real estate, the story's even tougher—vacancies are high, and investors are spooked. So, while rate cuts might slow the crash, they won't trigger a big rebound right away. It'll take time for confidence to return and for the dust to settle."

She added, "In short: lower rates are a lifeline, not a magic fix. The property market will eventually find its footing, but 2025 and even into 2026, it's going to be a cautious, slow recovery—more marathon than sprint."

I glanced at Lisa, curiosity getting the better of me. "What about inflation? Is the world headed for stagflation, or will things finally cool off?"

Lisa took a moment before answering, her tone thoughtful. "The consensus from the astrologers and psychics is that inflation remains stubbornly high through much of 2025—especially in the U.S. and Europe. Even with interest rate cuts later in the year, the effects of earlier supply chain shocks, tariffs, and wage pressures keep prices elevated. Food, energy, and basic goods are hit hardest."

I frowned. "So, does that mean we're stuck with high prices and slow growth?"

She nodded. "That's the risk. Several forecasts—including from astrology and mainstream analysts—warn that 2025 and even into 2026 could look a lot like stagflation: persistent inflation combined with sluggish or even negative growth. Unemployment ticks up, and real GDP growth slows to a crawl, especially in the U.S. and parts of Europe. It's not a runaway crisis, but it's a tough environment for both households and businesses."

I sighed. "So, no quick fix?"

Lisa smiled wryly. "Not this time. The stars suggest governments will try to stimulate growth with rate cuts and new spending, but the underlying issues—like debt, supply chain fragility, and global tensions—don't go away overnight. The advice is to stay cautious, keep an eye on essentials, and be ready for a slow, grinding recovery rather than a dramatic turnaround."

I glanced at Lisa as we walked, curiosity piqued. "What about tariffs? Are they going up, down, or just getting more complicated? And what impact do they actually have on all this economic drama?"

Lisa gave a knowing smile. "Tariffs are definitely a hot topic for 2025. The predictions—both astrological and psychic—show that while some of the emergency tariffs from recent years might come down a bit, they're not going away. Expect them to stay in the 10–20% range for many goods, especially anything connected to China or countries seen as strategic competitors."

I nodded. "So, even if they ease a little, we're still paying a premium at the store?"

"Exactly," she said. "And the impact is double-edged. On one hand, tariffs keep prices high for imports, which feeds into inflation—especially for things like electronics, cars, and household goods. On the other, they're supposed to protect domestic industries, but the reality is, companies like Walmart and Target can't just absorb those costs. They pass them on to us, the consumers, and that keeps the inflationary pressure going."

I frowned. "Does that mean we get any relief, or is it just a slow grind?"

Lisa shook her head. "It's mostly a slow grind. The Trump administration is predicted to keep tariffs as a bargaining chip in trade deals, especially with the UK, EU, and Asia. There's some relief in sight for a few sectors—like luxury cars from the UK might get exemptions—but for most everyday goods, the tariffs stick around. This means ongoing price hikes, supply chain headaches, and more pressure on household budgets."

She added, "And globally, tariffs spark a domino effect. The EU, China, and even India are expected to respond with their own tariffs or trade barriers. So, it's not just an American issue—it's a global tug-of-war that keeps costs high and growth slow in a lot of places. The advice? Expect trade friction to be a constant background noise through 2025 and into 2026."

I paused, then asked, "Lisa, is there anything in the predictions about the financial crisis that's truly unexpected? Something that would surprise even the skeptics?"

Lisa's eyes lit up with that mix of mischief and seriousness I'd come to expect. "Actually, yes—there are a few wildcards the predictions keep circling back to. For one, several psychics and astrologers foresee a major 'banking reset' moment in October 2025, where not only do dozens of small and mid-sized banks fail in the U.S., Europe and India, but there's talk of an overnight merger of banks—almost like a surprise musical chairs, with only the biggest banks left standing."

She continued, "Another curveball? There's a prediction that governments will use the crisis as the launchpad for rolling out central bank digital currencies much faster than anyone expects. The crash and the chaos could be the trigger for suddenly announcing a new digital dollar or euro, and even tying emergency aid or universal basic income to these new currencies."

I raised my eyebrows. "That's a big leap. Anything else?"

Lisa nodded. "Yes, and this one's really out there: some astrologers and psychics say the crash will expose hidden truths—not just about finances, but about elite corruption, shadow economies, and even suppressed tech disclosures. The idea is that the same period of financial collapse brings a wave of revelations that shake public trust in ways we haven't seen before. It's not just about money—it's about the whole system being forced into the open."

She grinned. "So, if you're expecting just another recession, you might want to buckle up. The predictions hint at a financial crisis that's not just about numbers, but about changing the rules of the game—and maybe even revealing a few secrets we never saw coming."

United Kingdom

As we finally settled into the patio, stretching our legs after the long trek, I let out a contented sigh. "You know, Lisa, it's amazing how far you can walk when you're out in nature and deep in conversation. I almost forgot we'd been gone for hours."

Lisa smiled, leaning back in her chair. "That's the magic of unplugging. Out here, the world's chaos feels a little less urgent."

I glanced at her, curiosity piqued. "So, let's talk about the UK. What's next for British politics? I keep hearing about shake-ups and surprises across the pond."

Lisa chuckled, swirling her glass. "Oh, the UK is in for quite a ride. The predictions—both psychic and astrological—say the political landscape is about to get a serious jolt. We already covered the first aspectThe Labor government is facing mounting economic chaos, and there's a strong chance Keir Starmer won't last the year as Prime Minister. There's even talk of Nigel Farage and the Reform Party gaining ground and possibly forming a coalition with the Conservatives, with Reform as the senior partner."

I raised an eyebrow. "So, Starmer's out and Farage is in? That's a big swing."

She nodded. "It is. The sense is that economic troubles—rising inflation, public sector strikes, and a housing crisis—will erode confidence in Labor. Rachel Reeves may also step down. The Conservatives are in disarray, but Farage's Reform is expected to capitalize on public frustration, especially if the cost-of-living crisis worsens and strikes keep paralyzing transport and the NHS."

I leaned forward, intrigued. "Does that mean Boris Johnson is out for good, or is there another comeback in the cards?"

Lisa grinned. "Don't count Boris out just yet. The predictions say his political career isn't over. There's a possibility he could return in some capacity, especially if the Tories need a charismatic figure to rally around. But the real headline is the rise of Reform and the possibility of a new coalition government that shakes up the status quo."

She paused, looking thoughtful. "And all this political turbulence is just the start. The UK's economy, housing, and public services are all set for a wild year. But one thing's for sure—British politics is about to get a whole lot livelier."

I set my pen down and flexed my aching hand, wincing. "Lisa, I think I've developed carpal tunnel just from trying to keep up with your predictions. At this rate, interviews with you are a medical hazard!" Lisa burst out laughing, nearly spilling her tea. "You think you've got it bad? My family says I should start handing out wrist braces with every reading. Maybe we should add a warning label: 'Caution—future forecasting may cause note-taking injuries!'" We both chuckled, letting the tension ease for a moment before I nudged us back to business. "Alright, let's give my hand a break from scribbling and talk about the UK—are they even relevant in this new world order, or are they just background noise?"

Lisa grinned, then grew thoughtful. "The UK is in a real crucible in 2025. Psychically and astrologically, it's a year of reckoning. The Labor government is teetering—Starmer faces mounting resignations, scandals, and a public that's losing patience with economic chaos: inflation, strikes, and a housing crisis that just won't quit. Predictions show Starmer likely won't last the year, and we could see the Reform Party—yes, Farage's crew—forming a coalition with the Conservatives, possibly even as the senior partner. That's a seismic shift. The UK's global relevance isn't what it was in the old days of empire, but it's not irrelevant either. Instead, Britain's role is becoming more reactive and pragmatic. They're scrambling to sign individual tariff deals to offset post-Brexit trade losses, but their leverage is diminished. Militarily, there are warnings of under-investment biting hard: a UK naval vessel could face a disaster due to lack of repairs, and cyberattacks on aviation and healthcare are likely. The psychic consensus is that the UK will be forced to adapt quickly—its voice still matters in Western alliances, but it's no longer the lead actor on the global stage. By early 2026, things begin to stabilize, but only after a political roller coaster and a bruised sense of national identity."

She glanced at her notes, her tone turning more somber. "And then there's the Royal Family. This is a year of shocks and transformation. At least two ceremonial funerals are predicted—a younger male royal, possibly involved in a travel incident, and a female royal with a history of health issues or medication. There's a major scandal brewing, targeting a woman in the family and involving money transfers, children, and underhanded tactics. King Charles himself faces additional health scares, and the monarchy is rocked by public debate about its future. The press will focus on the children of the deceased female royal, and family tensions will spill into the open. The psychic and astrological readings agree: 2025 brings a 'big, big shock change' to the monarchy, setting off a wave of transformation and public soul-searching. By 2026, the Royal Family's internal drama mirrors the UK's own struggle to redefine its place in a world that's moved on. The monarchy survives, but it's forced to adapt—just like the nation itself. So, is the UK still relevant? Absolutely—but only if it can reinvent itself, let go of old illusions, and embrace a new, more humble role in the global order."

"Okay, Lisa, let's talk about the UK and natural calamities. My hand can take a little more—what are the predictions for Britain in 2025?"

Lisa's expression grew serious as she sifted through her notes and memories from dozens of psychic, Vedic, and channeled readings. "This is one of those years where the UK faces a string of natural and man-made disasters—almost like the country is being tested on every front." She started ticking off the patterns. "First, the weather: 2025 is marked by extreme swings. There are repeated warnings about record-breaking heat waves, especially in late June and July. Astrologically, Mars in Leo is a classic signature for fire and drought, and the UK is flagged for its hottest summer on record, with water shortages and even talk of rationing by 2026. Some readings warn of a historic drought—reservoirs running dangerously low, hosepipe bans, and even the risk of wildfires in southern England, which is rare for the region."

She continued, "But it's not just heat. Several psychics see a pattern of sudden, violent storms and flash floods—especially in the north and Midlands. There's a strong theme of infrastructure being overwhelmed: rivers bursting their banks, roads and railways washed out, and even the London Underground facing closures due to electrical outages from flooding. One channeled prediction specifically mentions a 'major tunnel or bridge collapse' with UK connections, possibly linked to a combination of heavy rain and structural neglect. And then there's the cyber side: multiple sources warn of cyberattacks on the UK's energy and water grids, leading to rolling blackouts and disruptions in basic services. These outages could last for days in some regions, especially during the peak of summer demand."

Lisa paused, glancing at her tea. "There's also a maritime warning—psychics and remote viewers see a UK naval vessel running into serious trouble, possibly taking on water or even sinking due to underinvestment and lack of repairs. It's a wake-up call about old infrastructure and the dangers of cutting corners. And don't forget the aviation sector: a cyberattack or technical failure is predicted to ground flights at a major UK airport, causing chaos and stranding thousands.

Some see this as a catalyst for broader debates about national preparedness and resilience."

She leaned in, her tone softer. "And all of this is happening against a backdrop of mass awakening and social unrest. The predictions say that these calamities—whether natural or man-made—act as a trigger for a deeper reckoning within the UK. People are forced to band together, re-evaluate priorities, and demand accountability from leaders. The collective message from the psychics and astrologers is clear: the UK's challenges in 2025 are not just about surviving the storms, but about rediscovering community, resilience, and a sense of shared destiny in the face of upheaval."

I shook my hand out dramatically, pretending to grimace. Lisa burst out laughing, nearly snorting her tea. "Well, if you're looking for stock tips, maybe invest in wrist braces and ergonomic pens. The way things are going, those might be the only safe bets in 2025!"

We both chuckled, then I nudged the conversation back on track. "Alright, Lisa, let's talk turkey: What's happening with the UK economy and the share market this year? Should the Brits be stuffing cash under my mattress or buying the dip?"

Lisa grinned, but her eyes were serious. "The UK economy in 2025 is like a roller coaster designed by a committee—lots of twists, a few loops, and nobody's quite sure where the brakes are. Psychic and astrological predictions, as well as the consensus from our research, all point to a rough ride through the summer. Inflation remains stubbornly high, especially on essentials like food, utilities, and rent. Even as the Bank of England tries to cut rates, it's like putting a plaster on a leaky pipe: the underlying issues—supply chain chaos, energy shocks, and wage pressures—keep prices elevated."

She continued, "The share market is in for a wild time. There's a strong psychic consensus of a major global crash or at least a sharp correction between June and July 2025. The UK's FTSE isn't immune—expect big swings, with banking and property stocks especially vulnerable. Some astrologers even compare the setup to the 1929 crash, though this one is expected to be shorter: a deep drop, panic headlines, and then a surprisingly quick rebound within three weeks for the main indices. But the pain lingers for ordinary people—job losses, business closures, and a lot of anxiety about pensions and savings."

I raised an eyebrow. "So, is it all doom and gloom, or is there a silver lining?"

Lisa smirked. "Well, if you've got nerves of steel and a long-term horizon, the crash could be a buying opportunity—just don't expect instant gratification. The psychic and astrological patterns suggest the UK economy starts to stabilize by early 2026, but it's more of a slow grind than a V-shaped recovery. Unemployment ticks up, consumer confidence is shaky, and the government scrambles to patch holes with new spending and targeted relief. The advice from the spirit world? Keep your essentials covered, don't over-leverage, and maybe avoid betting the farm on meme stocks or crypto this summer."

She winked. "And if all else fails, invest in tea and biscuits. No matter how wild the markets get, the British will always need a good cuppa to get through the chaos!"

I asked, "Why does it feel like the UK is slipping down the world order these days?"

Lisa's smile faded into a thoughtful frown. "Honestly, it's a combination of everything hitting at once—psychic predictions, astrology, even the headlines all agree. The UK is being battered from all sides in 2025. Economically, inflation is stubborn, the cost-of-living crisis just won't quit, and there are constant warnings about banking and property shocks. But it's not just the numbers. The country's political system is in chaos: Starmer's government is on the ropes, with resignations and scandals piling up, and there's even talk of Reform forming a coalition with the Conservatives. That's a huge shake-up, and it's making the UK look unstable to the rest of the world."

I nodded, "But is it just politics and money, or is there something deeper going on?"

Lisa leaned in, lowering her voice. "It's deeper. The psychic and astrological consensus is that the UK is paying the price for years of underinvestment, division, and a refusal to adapt. There are repeated visions of strikes—transport, NHS, even teachers—paralyzing the country. Some even see violent protests erupting, especially if the government tries to push through austerity or controversial policies. And then you've got cyberattacks on aviation and healthcare, a possible naval disaster, and even a tunnel or bridge collapse. It's like every weak spot is being exposed at once."

I scribbled a few notes, then asked, "So, is the UK still relevant in the global order?"

Lisa shrugged. "Relevant, yes—but more as a cautionary tale than a leader. The UK is scrambling to sign new trade deals, but its leverage is weaker than ever. The psychic predictions say Britain's voice in Western alliances still matters, especially as the US pivots toward new partnerships, but it's no longer the first among equals. The next year is about survival and adaptation, not global leadership. There's a sense that by 2026, things stabilize a bit, but only after a wild political and social roller coaster."

She paused, then added, "And don't forget the Royal Family drama—two funerals, a major scandal, Charles's health scares. Even the monarchy is mirroring the country's uncertainty and need for reinvention. In a way, the UK's struggles are forcing it to finally confront what isn't working—and maybe, just maybe, to start writing a new story."

I asked, clicking the top of my ball pen, "Seems like a turbulent time."

Lisa stirred her tea thoughtfully. "The psychics and Vedic charts are remarkably unanimous on a looming crisis in the UK healthcare system," she began. "Between late July and early September 2025, there's a strong warning of a major cyber-attack that will cripple NHS networks—patient records will vanish, ambulance dispatchers won't get through, and some hospitals will be forced to divert emergency cases for days."

I frowned. "That's horrendous. And the public reaction?"

"Politically explosive. Multiple sources foresee nationwide strikes—rail workers, bus drivers, and even teachers walking out simultaneously in protest over government austerity and after repeated wage disputes. The Vedic nodal transit into Leo amplifies collective anger, making these walkouts among the most disruptive since 1979. Expect trains and tubes at a standstill for weeks, with Londoners walking to work through smoky underground tunnels turned into protest encampments."

"I have heard you say a lot about leaders facing issues. You talked about attempts on life, submarine issues and blackouts."

"Yes, a failed assassination attempt, likely on a major President, is flagged for late August 2025, with an "inside-job" scenario eerily reminiscent of a previous President shooting—no fatality but massive political fallout and emergency VP stepping up temporarily. In parallel, psychics vividly describe a submarine fire or explosion in the Red Sea around early September 2025, involving a nuclear-powered vessel near a major port city and a Western carrier group rushing to rescue wounded sailors."

Lisa leaned forward. "Don't overlook continental Europe. After the UK's NHS crisis, simultaneous blackouts strike Spain, Portugal, and southern France in mid-August 2025—cyber saboteurs target power grids under the guise of "solar storm" warnings. That sparks riots in Barcelona and Lyon, forcing EU ministers into emergency talks."

I nodded. "And politically?"

"Rising far-right parties exploit the chaos. Germany sees a surge in protest votes against Berlin's leadership, while Italy edges toward early elections as pensioners blockade highways. The karmic

Saturn–Neptune conjunction in Pisces exposes long-buried corruption, triggering mass resignations in several governments by autumn 2025."

"Lisa, that UK cyberattack sounds like a nightmare. How do people even cope?"

"They'll scramble back to paper charts, pen and paper, even carrier pigeons if need be. It's a wake-up call about digital overdependence—but also a trial by fire for community resilience."

"And the strikes—could they really paralyze a country this deep into summer?"

"The charts show Mars in Leo conjunct Ketu stirring a perfect storm of industrial unrest. Imagine West Ham supporters and bus drivers on the same picket lines—solidarity strike mania!"

"Sounds wild. But these events can't all be doom and gloom, right?"

"Exactly. Just as the NHS journalists hack uncovers hidden flaws, it also ignites public demand for reform. And the strikes—once the pain threshold is reached—open the door for new labor agreements and digital backup systems. Crisis births innovation."

I leaned forward with curiosity, "Lisa, these Digital Boroughs sound almost like sci-fi. Do you really see the UK embracing blockchain for local governance?"

Lisa smiled thoughtfully, "Absolutely. The psychics' visions weren't vague—they saw digital kiosks in town squares where residents scan a civic ID to cast votes on hyper-local issues. It's about reclaiming agency after years of feeling ignored by distant MPs. This isn't just technology for its own sake; it responds to a deeper yearning for community resilience in the face of political fragmentation."

"And the environmental triggers—funding garden projects when air quality dips—how does that work?" "That's the genius of it. Sensors across these boroughs feed data into public ledgers. If particulate levels rise, a smart contract releases funds automatically to green initiatives—tree planting, bike-lane creation, air-purifying mural projects. It flips the script on reactive policy by embedding collective well-being into the very fabric of governance."

I decided to put the pen down and rest for a bit. We had a few more topics and countries to cover.

Europe

Lisa and I settled in, the air heavy with the sense that Europe was at a crossroads. "Lisa, it feels like the Euro zone is under siege from every direction—war, economic shocks, even spiritual unrest. What are the big themes you're seeing in the predictions for Europe this year?" I asked, pen poised.

She nodded, her expression serious. "The psychic consensus is that 2025 is a year of reckoning for Europe. The most dramatic warnings foresaw a devastating conflict breaking out in Europe this year—one that could decimate populations and trigger a cascade of crises across the continent. Prophecies specifically mention a war that leaves Europe 'abandoned,' with mass migration, destruction, and a sense of the old order collapsing. Some predictions echo this, predicting 'cruel wars' and the return of an ancient plague, possibly a pandemic, that will test Europe's resilience to the core."

Lisa flipped through her notes. "It's not just the old prophecies. Modern psychics are also sounding the alarm. They see 2025 as the year when World War III could erupt, with Europe as the main battleground. The conflict is expected to be different from past wars—more cyber warfare, more religious and nationalist violence, and a sense that the continent is being pulled apart from within as much as from without. There's a strong theme of the UK being drawn into the conflict, and of Russia playing a dominant, even expansionist, role. Some channeled sources suggest that the US will be less reliable as an ally, forcing Europe to stand on its own and develop new forms of unity and strength".

She continued, "Economically, the psychic and astrological predictions are just as turbulent. The Euro is under pressure, with warnings of a slow recovery at best and a risk of further shocks if the war escalates or if US tariffs hit European exports. Germany, the traditional engine of the Euro zone, is seen as structurally weak, and there's concern that the manufacturing sector could be hit hard by both external trade wars and internal instability. Some astrologers even predict that the Euro will face trouble into 2026 and 2027, with the risk of financial crises and the possibility of the EU itself fracturing or transforming in response to these pressures".

Lisa leaned in, her voice lowering. "From a astrology perspective, 2025 is marked by Saturn's entry into Pisces—a major karmic shift. Saturn in Pisces is said to bring instability to financial and political structures, especially in Western nations. The combination of Saturn's discipline and Pisces' fluidity creates a push-pull effect: spiritual awakenings on one hand, but also the risk of economic downturns, social unrest, and even structural collapses in the Euro zone. The rare six-planet conjunction in Pisces this spring is seen as a trigger for global transformation, with Europe at the epicenter of these changes. The predictions warn of more water-related disasters—floods, storms, and even issues with shipping and trade. There's also a sense that the old order is being swept away, making room for new leaders and new forms of governance, possibly even a redrawing of the map in the years ahead".

sighed, scribbling furiously. "So, Lisa, is there any hope in all this? Or is it just doom and gloom for Europe?"

She smiled, a glimmer of optimism in her eyes. "Even the darkest predictions say that Europe's troubles are a catalyst for transformation. The psychic and astrological threads suggest that, while 2025 is brutal, it's also a turning point. There's a call for unity, for spiritual renewal, and for a return to core values—identity, autonomy, and community.

Some channeled sources even see Europe emerging stronger by 2026 or 2027, with new leadership, reformed institutions, and a more authentic sense of purpose. The message is clear: the old ways are ending, but what comes next is up to us. Europe's resilience, creativity, and capacity for reinvention are its greatest assets in this time of upheaval."

I couldn't help but joke, "Lisa, if French politics were a wine, would 2025 be a bold red or just a bottle of vinegar?".

Lisa grinned, "Definitely a blend—full-bodied, but with a sharp aftertaste! Psychic and astrological predictions for France in 2025 are all about turbulence and transformation. The country limps out of 2024 battered by two elections, four governments, and a deficit that's left even the European Commission clutching its pearls. The far-right party has surged to historic highs, while President Macron's centrist coalition has shrunk dramatically, leaving France with a hung parliament and a government that's about as stable as a Parisian soufflé in a thunderstorm. The snap legislative elections and the rise of Marine Le Pen have set the stage for ongoing parliamentary instability, with the threat of new elections always looming in the background."

Lisa sipped her tea and added, "Astrologers and psychics see 2025 as a year of civil unrest and political drama in France. The interior minister himself has warned of a 'highly inflammable' situation, with the risk of violence and protests running high—especially with the Paris Olympics adding extra fuel to the fire. There's talk of a potential immigration bill to appease the far-right, but that could backfire and trigger even more unrest. Meanwhile, Marine Le Pen is preparing for a possible snap presidential run, and both she and the new prime minister face legal clouds of their own. The psychic consensus? France's political scene is a powder keg, and the only certainty is more surprises ahead."

Lisa chuckled, "If Germany's politics were a car, 2025 is the year it goes in for a major tune-up—and maybe a new engine. Astrology and psychic predictions agree - Germany's federal elections in 2025 are a pivotal moment, with Saturn's transit signaling a phase of deep transformation. The country faces a tug-of-war between traditional values and progressive reforms, with far-right and far-left parties gaining traction as public discontent simmers. The astrological alignments suggest that debates around immigration, economic recovery, and national identity will intensify, and the outcome could swing between stricter policies or a renewed push for centrist, inclusive governance.

Lisa pointed out, "The psychic and astrological consensus is that Germany's next government could be a wild card—anything from a rightward shift to an unconventional coalition. The presence of Mars and the lunar nodes in the national chart hints at passionate debates, surprise alliances, and a possible rise of new political movements. Whatever happens, Germany's choices will ripple across Europe, affecting everything from EU stability to global trade. The advice from the stars? Stay flexible, expect the unexpected, and keep an eye on those coalition talks."

Lisa laughed, "Italy's politics are like a soap opera—just when you think you know the plot, someone new walks in with a dramatic monologue! Psychic and astrological predictions for Italy in 2025 highlight ongoing populist currents and a restless electorate. The right-wing coalition is riding high. The psychic consensus is that Italy will continue to see political fragmentation, with new parties and alliances forming as old ones fade. The risk of snap elections or government collapses remains high, and the country's relationship with the EU is under constant negotiation."

Lisa added, "Astrologers see Italy's chart as full of tension—Mars and Saturn suggest a year of heated debates over economic reforms, immigration, and national identity. The stars warn of more protests and public unrest, especially if austerity measures or unpopular reforms are pushed through. But there's also a chance for renewal: if Italy can channel its creative chaos, it might just surprise everyone with a new wave of pragmatic, reformist leadership. Either way, expect plenty of drama—and maybe a few plot twists worthy of a Roman epic."

I asked Lisa to wait - she was speaking too fast and my notes had to catch up. I didn't want to miss anything. It is tough to do true psychic reading and according to Lisa, electronics, especially cell towers, interfered with her ability to focus.

Lisa grinned, "Spain in 2025 is like a tapas bar—lots of small plates, but everyone's arguing over the bill!" Psychic predictions for Spain this year have been uncannily specific: they accurately foresaw the massive blackouts that hit Spain and Portugal in April, describing them as a rehearsal for more widespread disruptions. These outages, attributed to cyber-warfare, plunged cities into chaos and highlighted the vulnerability of modern infrastructure. The psychic warning is clear: Spain's political environment will be shaped by ongoing unrest, protests, and the ever-present risk of further disruptions to daily life.

Lisa continued, "On the political front, Spain faces mass protests and calls for Prime Minister Pedro Sanchez to resign over corruption scandals. The right-wing Popular Party is capitalizing on public anger, and the government is under pressure from both economic challenges and a series of high-profile investigations. Astrologers see Saturn's influence as a test of resilience, with the potential for snap elections or a major political shake-up if the unrest continues. The advice? Keep your candles handy—and maybe a protest sign, just in case."

"What about the rest of Europe?"

Lisa sighed, "The Rest of Europe - Populism, Protests, and the Great Recalibration".

Lisa leaned back, "If you think the rest of Europe is any calmer, think again. The psychic and astrological consensus is that 2025 is a year of recalibration across the continent. Populist and far-right parties are gaining ground in countries like Poland, Hungary, and Romania, often fueled by economic grievances, immigration debates, and a backlash against EU policies. The European Parliament elections and a slew of national votes are testing the old 'firewall' that kept extremists out of power, and coalition governments are more fragile than ever."

She added, "Astrologers see the rare planetary alignments of 2025 as a catalyst for deep change—expect more protests, strikes, and political volatility, especially in response to austerity, climate policies, and foreign affairs. The EU itself is at a crossroads, with rising nationalism and economic pressures threatening to fracture the union or force a major transformation. The advice from the stars and the psychics? Stay nimble, keep your passport up to date, and don't be surprised if the political map looks very different by the end of the year."

"What about the economy and stock market?"

"It's not very different than what you can see for the US. A major correction or crash. A "historic" drop, likened to past crashes, but short-lived (roughly two to three weeks). Recovery begins by late July or August, as Jupiter's sign changes and Mars exits stress aspects to Saturn. Banking, property, and highly leveraged tech and crypto assets are expected to suffer the deepest declines during the crash window. Predicted flare-ups (e.g., Middle East incidents) could trigger sell-offs as risk appetite wanes."

I poured myself a coffee and glanced at Lisa. "Alright, Lisa, let's tackle Europe. Is the continent still the 'sick man' of the global economy, or is there a pulse under all that pessimism?"

Lisa grinned. "It's complicated, but there's more life than most people think. Inflation is finally cooling, with eurozone rates expected to be more stabke in 2026. Unemployment is holding steady despite all the global drama. So, it's not a roaring recovery, but it's a lot sturdier than the headlines suggest".

She continued, "The big drag is trade uncertainty. The U.S. tariffs and global supply chain headaches have forced a downgrade in growth forecasts, and there's a real risk that things could get worse if trade disputes escalate. But there are bright spots: predictions are for fiscal stimulus in Germany, deregulation efforts in Brussels, and a wave of infrastructure and defense spending are all helping to offset the gloom. The IMF and European Commission both say the risks are tilted to the downside, but if Europe can keep its markets open and push through reforms, there's a real chance for a stronger rebound in 2026".

I leaned in, curious. "So, what about the stock market? Is Europe still playing second fiddle to the U.S., or is there a changing of the guard?"

Lisa smiled. "This year has been a real plot twist. European stocks have outperformed U.S. equities for the first time in years. That's the widest gap in decades, and it's drawing in value investors from around the world. I think there will be continued interest in Europe."

She added, "The sector story is key. Europe is less tech-heavy than the U.S. Instead, Europe is loaded with financials, industrials, energy, and consumer stocks. In 2025, financials and industrials will lead the way, with banks, aerospace, and logistics companies posting double-digit gains. Utilities, real estate, and defense are also in the spotlight, thanks to fiscal stimulus and higher government spending. Meanwhile, tech has lagged, but there are signs of a rebound as global supply chains stabilize and U.S.-China trade tensions ease. The psychic consensus is that the economy will start to recover only after the political shift, with the Sun's influence in the national chart supporting a slow rebound in late 2025 and into 2026. Until then, expect continued stagnation, labor unrest, and a cautious investment climate. While Spain will avoid recession, growth will gradually lose momentum as global trade uncertainty and tariffs weigh on exports and investment. Public finances remain vulnerable, and there's a need for consensus on long-term reforms to boost productivity and labor market participation"

I joked,"I see you have some finance clients, Lisa. You sound like a finance newscaster."

Lisa smiled. It was her rule not to discuss clients. Apart from some playful comments like this one, we never discussed her clients.

Me: "And what about the weather and natural calamities?"

Lisa: "France, like much of Europe, is flagged for climate extremes this year. Several modern psychic predictions warn of 'the dry Earth becoming more parched and great floods'—so expect a summer of droughts punctuated by sudden, severe flooding. There's also a psychic warning about the return of ancient plagues or pestilence, which could be literal (like a disease outbreak) or symbolic of social unrest. The overall message is to prepare for volatility, both economically and in the environment, with resilience and adaptability as the best strategies. Germany is flagged for severe weather events in 2025. Vedic and psychic sources highlight the risk of major flooding, especially in central and eastern regions, as well as possible droughts in the north. There's also a warning about infrastructure being overwhelmed—rivers bursting their banks, and even the risk of a tunnel or bridge collapse. The psychic consensus is that these events will act as a wake-up call for investment in resilience and climate adaptation, but the immediate impact will be disruptive "

"What about Spain?", I asked, trying to keep up.

"Spain is flagged for extreme weather—especially heatwaves and drought in the south and east, with the risk of wildfires. Psychic predictions also warn of sudden, violent storms and flash floods, particularly in the north and along the Mediterranean coast. There's a strong theme of infrastructure being tested, with the potential for transport and energy disruptions. The advice is to prepare for a year of climate extremes, but also to see these challenges as catalysts for innovation and community resilience. Same with Italy. Italy is flagged for a mix of drought and flooding, especially in the north. Psychic and astrological sources warn of a hot, dry summer with water shortages, followed by sudden storms and the risk of landslides in mountainous regions. There's also a warning about seismic activity—earthquakes are always a risk in Italy, and 2025 is seen as a year to be vigilant, especially in central and southern regions. The overall message is to invest in resilience and be prepared for rapid shifts in weather patterns."

"Lisa, let's zoom out. What's the big picture for the eurozone as a whole?"

"The eurozone faces a challenging year. Psychic and astrological sources see the main drag coming from trade policy uncertainty, high energy prices, and structural headwinds in manufacturing. The services sector is more resilient, but consumer confidence is fragile and saving rates are high. The psychic consensus is that the eurozone will avoid recession, but growth will be modest and uneven, with the south (Spain, Italy) outperforming the north (Germany, France). There's also a warning about financial market volatility, with the risk of sudden shocks from global events or policy missteps. The advice is to stay flexible, diversify investments, and be prepared for a year of surprises."

Me: "And what about natural calamities across the region?"

"Europe as a whole is flagged for a year of climate extremes—heatwaves, droughts, floods, and storms. Psychic and Vedic sources warn of a 'year of reckoning' for the continent, with infrastructure and emergency services being tested by back-to-back disasters. There's also a warning about the risk of disease outbreaks, either literal (like a new pandemic) or symbolic of social and political unrest. The overall message is to invest in resilience, strengthen community ties, and be ready to adapt to rapidly changing conditions. Predictions also foresee unprecedented solar activity, with flares disrupting technology, communications, and power grids. These flares are said to trigger natural disasters and societal upheaval, particularly in technologically advanced regions like Europe."

Australia

I plopped down on Lisa's couch, mug in hand. "Alright, Lisa, let's talk Australia. Should I be worried about bushfires, cyclones, or just running out of Tim Tams this year?" Lisa grinned, "Honestly, you might want to stock up on both Tim Tams and sunscreen. 2025 is shaping up to be a wild ride—weather, economy, and all. But hey, at least we'll have some beautiful sunsets to enjoy while the world goes bonkers!"

"Let's do a rapid fire session on Australia.", I said, hoping to speed up the interview.

Me:"So, what's the weather drama this year? Should I invest in an ark or a fire bunker?"

Lisa:"Both, if you can! Psychic and astrological predictions agree: 2025 brings more weather extremes. We're talking major flooding in some regions, but also record-breaking heat and bushfires—especially in places like Sydney and the Blue Mountains. There's even a vision of a tall tower burning in Sydney, with eucalyptus trees exploding in the heat. Authorities might just throw up their hands and say, 'Too hard, mate!'"

Me:"Exploding gum trees? That's so Australian. What about cyclones?"

Lisa:"Northern Australia's in for a soggy time—above-average rainfall and a higher risk of cyclones, especially in the Top End and far north Queensland. "

Me:"And earthquakes? Or is that just New Zealand's thing?"

Lisa:"Actually, Vedic astrology and some channeled predictions flag the northern part of Australia for possible earthquakes and mining disasters. Not the norm, but 2025 isn't a normal year. And don't get me started on the 'things falling from the sky'—satellites, space junk, you name it. If you see a Starlink satellite plummeting, just wave and say, 'Welcome to Oz!'"

Me:"Alright, Lisa, level with me. Is the economy as cooked as a Christmas prawn on Bondi Beach?"

Lisa:"Let's just say, don't quit your day job. Psychic Rose Smith warns that 2025 is stressful for most Aussies—lots of businesses could go under, and the average person is struggling. Inflation, rising prices, and unemployment are top concerns. The economy's not technically in recession, but it might feel like it's underwater—literally and figuratively, if those sea levels at Circular Quay keep rising!"

Me: "So, should I stuff cash under my mattress or invest in kangaroo futures?"

Lisa: "Maybe invest in a good sense of humor! The government's trying to help, but a lot of the pain is global—macroeconomic factors, not just local politics. Psychic forecasts say foreign trade slows, inflation bites, and there's a scarcity in national food reserves. But hey, at least the sunsets will be gorgeous—end of a chapter, as Rose puts it. And if all else fails, you can always barter Tim Tams for petrol."

Me:"What's the mood? Are Aussies still the world's chillest people, or are we all about to lose our cool?"

Lisa:"It's a mixed bag. There's a sense of resilience—Australia's starting a new 12-year cycle, so there's hope and creativity, but also disruption and a need for strong leadership. The psychic consensus is that Aussies will keep their sense of humor, even as reality bites. Expect more protests, strikes, and a bit of political rabble—maybe even some childlike behavior from the politicians. But there's also a call for

Australia to be the voice of reason and common sense on the world stage. So, chin up, mate!"

Me:"Any good news, or is it all doom and gloom?"

Lisa:"There's always a silver lining. Australia's in a position to learn from other countries' mistakes—forewarned is forearmed. And if you're feeling down, just remember: at least we're not dealing with snowstorms and alligators. Unless, of course, the next cyclone brings a few crocs to Sydney Harbour. Now that would be a headline!"

Me: "Lisa, if I see a kangaroo surfing a flood wave, should I take a photo or just join in?"

Lisa: "Definitely take the photo—then sell it to the tabloids! And if you see a koala with an umbrella, you'll know the weather's really gone troppo. Just remember, in Australia, if it's not the weather, it's the wildlife. Or the politicians. Or both at once!"

Canada

I set my mug down, flexing my hand. "Lisa, I feel like every time we talk about Canada, I need a double shot of espresso. The news is wild, the charts are wild, and now the psychic predictions are wild too. Is it just me, or does 2025 feel like a year where Canada's on a rollercoaster with no brakes?"

Lisa grinned. "You're not wrong. The psychic and astrological signals for Canada this year are all over the map—literally and figuratively. Let's break it down, one headline at a time."

Economic Outlook: Wild Ride, Resilience, and Uncertainty

Me: "Let's start with the economy. Are we in for a crash, a boom, or just more confusion?"

Lisa: "The consensus is: buckle up. Psychics and astrologers agree that 2025 is a year of economic turbulence for Canada. There's a 'rollercoaster' theme—periods of growth and optimism, but also sharp downturns and uncertainty, especially tied to US tariffs and global trade wars. The Canadian dollar is predicted to strengthen, possibly even reaching parity with the US dollar, which could boost purchasing power for Canadians. But the threat of US tariffs looms large, creating volatility and forcing Canadian businesses to adapt quickly to changing market conditions. The psychic vision shows a surge in technological innovation, especially in cryptocurrency and AI, with Bitcoin and Ethereum predicted to reach new heights. For everyday Canadians, this means more tech jobs, increased interest in crypto, and a need for financial flexibility to weather the changes".

Me: "But what about jobs? I keep seeing headlines about unemployment."

Lisa: "That's the shadow side. Despite the optimism, the reality is that unemployment has surged—especially for young Canadians. The job market is the bleakest it's been in decades for recent graduates, with joblessness for this group hitting a two-decade high. The slow job growth and rising unemployment are directly tied to the US-Canada trade war, which has made it even harder for young people to enter the workforce. Economists warn that graduating during an economic downturn can have lasting effects, delaying early career progress and income growth. The psychic advice? Stay adaptable, learn new skills—especially in tech and AI—and be ready for a long game, not a quick fix".

Political and Social Atmosphere: Shifts, Unrest, and Innovation

Me: "So, is the political scene as wild as the economy?"

Lisa: "Wilder, if you can believe it. Psychic and astrological predictions point to a seismic political shift in 2025. There's a strong chance of a change in leadership, with a right-wing, populist leader foreseen to take the helm. This could mean major policy changes, a potential overhaul of immigration policies, and a focus on boosting housing supply. The new leadership is expected to challenge many existing policies, sparking intense political debate and even social unrest. Canadians can expect heated discussions on social media, increased political engagement among younger voters, and a surge in grassroots activism. The psychic consensus is that this period will encourage more Canadians to get involved in shaping the nation's future".

Me: "And what about the general mood? Are people hopeful or just exhausted?"

Lisa: "It's a mix. There's a sense of fatigue from years of economic and political uncertainty, but also a growing resolve and even optimism. Canadians are predicted to embrace change with resilience, especially as new opportunities emerge in tech, green energy, and cultural innovation. Indigenous communities are expected to become new power players, not just in culture but also in business, leading to a deeper national conversation about reconciliation and a revival of traditional crafts and skills. The overall mood is one of transformation—challenging, but ultimately strengthening".

US-Canada Relations: Tension, Trade Wars, and the Search for Balance

Me: "Lisa, I have to ask—how bad is it with the US? Are we really at risk of a trade war, or is it just more political theater?"

Lisa: "It's not just theater. The astrological and psychic signals show that US-Canada relations are under real strain in 2025. Trump's return to power has brought renewed threats of tariffs—up to 25% on all Canadian goods—and even talk of Canada becoming the '51st state' if it can't handle the economic fallout. The charts show Trump's influence as both disruptive and larger-than-life, with a focus on aggrandizing himself and using tariffs as leverage. This has created economic uncertainty, especially for Canadian exports like steel, aluminum, and automobiles. The psychic consensus is that while the relationship is tense, Canada will not be subsumed or broken. Instead, the country is predicted to adapt, find new markets, and strengthen alliances with Europe and other partners. There's also a strong theme of Canada asserting its sovereignty and identity, even as it navigates the turbulence".

Me: "So, is there any hope for a diplomatic breakthrough?"

Lisa: "Actually, yes. Some psychic visions point to a diplomatic breakthrough later in the year, with successful renegotiation of tariffs and improved trade relations. Canada's new leadership—whether current or a Conservative—will play a crucial role in mending fences and elevating Canada's standing on the global stage. But the process will be messy, with plenty of political drama and public debate along the way".

Election Drama and Economic Shifts

Me: "What do the Vedic and mundane astrologers say about all this?"

Lisa: "The Vedic New Year chart for Canada in 2025 shows a leadership crisis and the likely fall of the incumbent government. The stars suggest that the opposition Conservative Party could form a new government with the help of smaller parties, after a hung parliament. The economic outlook is mixed: while there are signs of growth and innovation, there are also warnings about financial instability, especially tied to global trade wars and the end of old trade agreements by 2029-2030. The astrological advice is to stay flexible, avoid binding agreements, and be ready for sudden changes in the economic landscape. The period from April 2025 to April 2026 is highlighted as the last 'rollercoaster' of economic upheaval, with a more stable period expected after 2026".

Me: "So, Lisa, if you had to sum up Canada's 2025 in a sentence?"

Lisa: "It's a year of turbulence and transformation. The economy is a wild ride, politics are in flux, and US-Canada relations are tense—but there's resilience, innovation, and a chance for renewal if Canadians stay adaptable and engaged. The psychic and astrological signals say: expect the unexpected, but don't lose hope. Canada's story isn't over—it's just turning a new page".

China

Setting the Scene: A Pause Before the Storm

I poured myself a cup of tea and glanced at Lisa. "Lisa, every time we talk about China, it feels like we're peering into a pressure cooker. The headlines are wild, the charts are wild, and now the psychic predictions are wild too. Is 2025 really the year China's economic story takes a sharp turn?"

Lisa grinned, but her eyes were serious. "If you're looking for a year of shocks, 2025 is it. The psychic, astrological, and channeled signals for China are all over the map—literally and figuratively. Let's break it down, one headline at a time."

The Big Picture: Economic Shockwaves and Uncertainty

Me: "Let's start with the economy. Are we talking about a crash, a boom, or just more confusion?"

Lisa: "The consensus is: buckle up. Multiple psychic and astrological sources predict a 'huge economic shock' for China in May 2025, described as an 'electrical storm'—possibly with real storms, but definitely with financial and social upheaval. This is the climax of a long cycle, which astrologers say is about the world economy turning upside-down. The period from April 2025 to April 2026 is the last wild ride of this cycle, and it's compared to the Great Depression and the Second World War, but with a modern twist: instead of a world war, we're in a global trade war, with tariffs, supply chain chaos, and currency volatility. The advice is to stay flexible, avoid binding agreements, and be ready for sudden changes in the economic landscape".

Me: "So, is there a specific window when things get really dicey?"

Lisa: "Yes. The most sensitive periods are late April through July 2025, with a cluster of astrological aspects that have historically coincided with market crashes and recessions. The risk of a recession or even a crash is highest from mid-June through late July, with echoes of the 1929 crash and other historic downturns. After that, things remain volatile, but the worst of the storm should pass by Easter 2026, when Uranus finally leaves Taurus for good".

Psychic and Channeled Warnings: Rebellion, Upheaval, and Social Strain

Me: "What about the social mood? Is it just economic, or is there something deeper going on?"

Lisa: "It's deeper. Psychic predictions and channeled sources foresee a period of rebellion and unrest in China, especially in the leadership ranks and on the streets. The Tarot and astrology both point to a 'volcanic' eruption—possibly literal, but definitely symbolic—of pent-up frustration. There's talk of a karmic reckoning, with echoes of the Taiping Rebellion and the Opium Wars. The psychic consensus is that July August 2025 brings a big shock, with the potential for protests, leadership upheaval, and a sense of the old order being challenged. The mood is anxious, volatile, and full of possibility for transformation".

Me: "So, is this the start of a revolution?"

Lisa: "Not a bloody revolution, but a powerful, sometimes violent move by the people against corruption and the new wealth. The move for democracy is seen as coming from within, possibly even from Maoist factions. There's also a spiritual dimension: as the economic machine slows, there's a predicted resurgence of Taoism, Feng Shui, and Chinese astrology, with people seeking meaning beyond material gains".

War, Recession, and Leadership Crisis

Me: "So, is there a risk of open conflict?"

Lisa: "Yes, especially in the second half of 2025 and into 2026. The charts show aggressive military moves, particularly in coordination with Pakistan against India, and the risk of border clashes and diplomatic isolation. The economic strain is compounded by these external pressures, and the leadership is seen as barely surviving amidst instability".

US-China Relations: Trade War, Tariffs, and Global Tension

Me: "Lisa, what about the US? Are we really at risk of a trade war, or is it just more political theater?"

Lisa: "It's not just theater. The astrological and psychic signals show that US-China relations are under real strain in 2025. The economic shock in May 2025 is directly linked to US tariffs and China's response. The period is described as the 'end of globalization,' with both sides launching new tariffs and trade restrictions. The psychic consensus is that the trade war is the modern equivalent of a world war—disruptive, but not apocalyptic. The US is predicted to reimpose tariffs exceeding 60% on direct Chinese exports, while China responds by limiting US access to critical minerals and tightening export controls. The result is a tit-for-tat trade war, with both economies suffering and global supply chains in chaos".

Me: "Does this spill over into other areas?"

Lisa: "Absolutely. The trade war is just the tip of the iceberg. There are warnings about cyberattacks, technology restrictions, and even the risk of military misadventures in the South China Sea or around Taiwan. The psychic and astrological consensus is that the US and China are locked in a strategic competition that will define the next decade, with 2025 as a turning point".

The General Atmosphere: Anxiety, Adaptation, and Spiritual Awakening

Me: "So, what's the mood in China? Are people hopeful or just exhausted?"

Lisa: "It's a mix. There's a sense of fatigue from years of economic and political uncertainty, but also a growing resolve and even optimism. As the economic machine slows, there's a predicted resurgence of traditional spirituality—Taoism, Feng Shui, and Chinese astrology. People are seeking meaning beyond material gains, and there's a sense that the old ways are ending, but what comes next is up to them. The psychic consensus is that China will become a happier country in the long run, with a new form of democratic capitalism and a spiritual renaissance. But 2025 is a crucible—a year of reckoning, transformation, and the possibility of a new beginning".

Lisa leaned back, her tone thoughtful. "China's official numbers may look stable, but the reality is a lot more fragile. The next year is about survival, adaptation, and preparing for a new chapter—one that could bring both challenges and opportunities for millions of Chinese workers and their families."

Latin America

Setting the Scene: A Pause for Perspective

I set my notebook down and stretched my hand. "Lisa, every time we get to Latin America, I feel like I need a double espresso and a world map. There's so much happening—politics, economics, even spiritual shifts. Is 2025 really as pivotal for the region as everyone says?"

Lisa grinned. "Absolutely. Latin America is at a crossroads this year—economically, politically, and even spiritually. The psychic, astrological, and channeled signals are all over the map, but some clear themes are emerging. Let's break it down country by country, and then look at the region as a whole."

Regional Overview: Modest Growth, High Uncertainty

Me: "Instead, let's start with the big picture. What's the overall economic mood for Latin America in 2025?"

Lisa: "The consensus is: modest growth, but with a lot of headwinds. Most forecasts—psychic, astrological, and mainstream—see the region growing below the global average. Inflation is finally cooling, and central banks are cautiously easing rates, but the region is still wrestling with high public debt, weak currencies, and the fallout from global trade tensions—especially US tariffs and the ongoing US-China rivalry. There's also a spiritual undertone: many psychics and channeled sources see 2025 as a year of reckoning and transformation, with old systems breaking down and new opportunities emerging for those who can adapt."

Country Snapshots: Winners, Losers, and Wild Cards

Argentina: From Crisis to Comeback

Me: "Argentina's been in the headlines for years. Is 2025 finally the turnaround?"

Lisa: "It looks that way. Psychic and economic forecasts both point to Argentina as the region's breakout story. After years of recession and runaway inflation, the country is expected to see real growth —the highest in Latin America. The key is the lifting of currency controls and a flood of foreign investment, which should boost the peso and make Argentina a hot market for global exporters. President Milei's radical reforms are paying off, and even though the pain has been real for ordinary Argentines, the mood is shifting from despair to cautious optimism. There's even talk of a 'libertarian revolution' spreading across the region, echoing the Menem-Cavallo reforms of the 1990s."

Brazil: Growth Amidst Political Gridlock

Me: "What about Brazil? It's always the regional heavyweight."

Lisa: "Brazil is growing, but not as fast as it could. The economy should expand, helped by a strong crop year and rising oil production. But the real is weak, public debt is very high, and President Lula is struggling to get anything through Congress. The psychic consensus is that Brazil is at risk of a currency crisis if it doesn't get its fiscal house in order. There's also tension with the US over trade—especially if Trump's tariffs hit Brazilian exports like ethanol, sugar, and industrial goods. The spiritual undertone is one of frustration: Brazil has the resources and talent to lead, but political misalignment is holding it back."

Mexico: Squeezed by Two Populists

Me: "Mexico seems caught between a rock and a hard place—what's the outlook?"

Lisa: "Mexico faces at least two years of economic struggle. Outgoing President's interference in energy and other sectors scared off over $100 billion in capital, and now Trump's tariff threats are adding more uncertainty. The trade agreement is up for renewal, and there's a real risk it could be renegotiated or even lapse, which would be a blow to investor confidence. Psychic and astrological sources warn of a 'hard reset' for Mexico's export-driven economy, but there's a silver lining: the need to align with US interests could spur a wave of domestic investment in manufacturing, especially as companies look to nearshore away from China. The mood is anxious but pragmatic—Mexico will adapt, but it won't be easy."

Chile, Colombia, and Peru: Commodity Cycles and Political Shifts

Me: "How about the Andean countries—Chile, Colombia, Peru?"

Lisa: "Chile and Colombia are both expected to grow around 2.4%, with Peru a bit higher. Chile is a bright spot for equities, thanks to strong earnings growth and a likely political shift to the center-right later in the year. But all three are vulnerable to global commodity cycles and US-China trade tensions. Peru's exports are at record highs, but political instability and organized crime are big challenges. Colombia's president is a lame duck, but the country's institutions are strong, and a younger population gives it long-term potential. Psychic and astrology sources see these countries as 'pivot points'—if they can weather the storms, they could emerge stronger by 2026."

Guyana and the Caribbean: Oil Boom and Tourism Rebound

Me: "Any outliers or surprises?"

Lisa: "Guyana is the region's superstar, with high GDP growth thanks to its oil boom. The Caribbean is also bouncing back, with tourism at record highs and sound governance in places like Jamaica and the Bahamas. The psychic consensus is that these countries are riding a wave of good fortune, but political violence or natural disasters could still derail progress. There's also a spiritual theme: the region is seen as a place of renewal and healing, especially as more people turn to traditional faiths and community rituals for support."

Bolivia, Ecuador, and the "Ugly" List

Me: "And the trouble spots?"

Lisa: "Bolivia is facing an economic mess—currency overvalued, gas and lithium industries underdeveloped, and political risk high. Ecuador is struggling with organized crime and a weak dollarized economy. Both are vulnerable to external shocks and could see more instability if global conditions worsen. Psychic and channeled sources warn of 'hidden dangers'—corruption, crime, and the risk of social unrest if reforms stall."

Spiritual and Cultural Atmosphere: A Year of Reckoning and Renewal

Me: "Lisa, what about the spiritual or cultural side? Any unique predictions for Latin America?"

Lisa: "Absolutely. 2025 is seen as a year of spiritual reckoning and renewal across the region. In Cuba, for example, the Yoruba priests' Letter of the Year predicts 'firm and secure health on the earth plane,' with Shango—deity of thunder, fire, and justice—reigning over 2025. This signals a year of passion, transformation, and the need for balance between power and compassion. Across Latin America, there's a renewed interest in traditional faiths, rituals, and community resilience. Psychics and channeled sources see a 'collective awakening'—people turning to local solutions, mutual aid, and spiritual practices to weather economic and social storms."

Key Themes and Risks for 2025

I mentioned to Lisa that I had one country and two major themes to cover yet so she gave me a handwritten sheet with some specific themes for Latin America. We are replicating the list here.

Trade and Tariffs: US tariffs and global trade fragmentation are the biggest external risks, especially for Mexico, Brazil, and Chile. Countries with diversified trade partners and strong institutions will fare better.

Currency and Debt: Weak currencies and high public debt are major vulnerabilities. Countries with sound fiscal management (like the Dominican Republic and Jamaica) are better positioned to weather shocks.

Commodities and Climate: The region's fortunes still rise and fall with commodity prices—copper, oil, soybeans, lithium. Climate change and extreme weather events (droughts, floods, cyclones) are growing threats, especially for agriculture and food security.

Crime and Governance: Organized crime and corruption remain persistent challenges, draining resources and undermining trust. Psychic and channeled sources warn of "hidden dangers" and the need for vigilance and reform.

Spiritual Resilience: There's a strong theme of spiritual renewal—people turning to faith, ritual, and community to find meaning and support. The year is seen as a turning point, with the potential for both crisis and transformation.

India and Asia

Setting the Scene: A Year of Reckoning

"Lisa, every time we talk about India, it feels like the country is standing at the crossroads of destiny—economically, politically, and spiritually. Is 2025 really as pivotal as the predictions say?"

Lisa replied, "Absolutely. The signals from Vedic astrology, psychic forecasts, and even ancient prophecies all point to 2025 as a year of profound transformation for India."

"Let's start with the economy. Are we looking at a boom, a bust, or just more volatility?"

"The mainstream numbers are still strong. But the psychic and astrological consensus is more nuanced. The year starts with optimism, but by mid-year, the planetary alignments signal a period of economic turbulence and market shocks."

"What's the trigger for the volatility?"

"The big astrological red flags -these are classic markers for financial instability, sudden corrections, and even a potential crash in the stock market. The period from late March through July is especially sensitive, with warnings of sharp corrections, high speculation, and deceptive rallies—particularly in tech, crypto, and overbought stocks. Prophecies warn of a global economic crisis, with money and gold losing value and essential goods becoming unaffordable."

"Does the market recover, or is this the start of a deeper crisis?"

"The consensus is that the worst volatility is short-lived—markets may rebound by late summer or early autumn, but the pain for ordinary people lingers: job losses, business closures, and anxiety about savings. The real risk is a slow grind of inflation and unemployment, especially for young people and those in the informal sector."

"What about politics? Is the government stable, or are we in for more drama?"

"2025 is a year of political firefighting. The astrological charts show the Sun as both king and prime minister, which means decisions are likely to be self-centered, top-down, and sometimes out of touch with public sentiment. There's tension between the central government and the states, with coalition partners threatening to withdraw support and the risk of instability rising toward the end of the year and into 2026. Psychic and channeled sources warn of a leadership crisis by late 2026, with the possibility of the current leader stepping down or being forced out before completing their term."

"Let's talk about the weather. Are we in for more climate chaos?"

"Absolutely. 2025 is flagged as a year of extreme weather. Psychics foresee unprecedented heat spikes across northern India during summer 2025; prolonged drought conditions threaten water supplies and agriculture. Threatens reservoirs and wildfires in Central India. Channeled predictions describe an erratic monsoon: torrential downpours alternated with dry spells, causing flash floods in Bihar and Assam by July 2025; riverbanks in Ganges and Brahmaputra basins are expected to breach, inundating villages and displacing thousands. Psychics warn of an unusually severe Bay of Bengal cyclone in October 2025, striking Odisha and Andhra Pradesh coasts with Category 4 strength, followed by storm surges up to 5 m high and extended power outages. Channeled visions also predict moderate earthquakes (magnitude 6–7) hitting the Himalayan foothills in mid-2025, affecting Uttarakhand and Himachal Pradesh; landslides will block key transit routes and strain rescue operations."

"Wow! And that is only India?"

"I haven't focused on Asia as much. But all predictions envision a tsunami in July 2025 for coastal Thailand and Myanmar, with waves up to 10 m tall produced by undersea tremors in Andaman Sea; harbors are predicted to face catastrophic inundation. Remote channels describe "water drawing back" phenomena preceding the tsunami, giving mere minutes for coastal residents to flee to higher ground. It is either the highest Tsunami recorded or a precursor to a major Tsunami event in South Asia."

Lisa sighed and was quiet for a bit.

"Channeled accounts forecast extreme flash floods in Vietnam during August 2025 as heavy monsoon rains overload dams; rice paddies and urban districts could be submerged waist-deep. Inundation events in Bangkok and surrounding provinces, warning of infrastructure collapse and waterborne disease outbreaks. Psychics also predict renewed activity at Mount Merapi (Indonesia) by late 2025, with ash columns reaching 15 km; Jakarta and Kuala Lumpur air traffic face prolonged closures, impacting the regional economy. There are a series of volcanic tremors leading to flows down Java's slopes, endangering nearby villages and requiring mass evacuations."

"Anything else? Things seem bleak enough."

"Yes. There's a warning about waterborne and respiratory diseases, with a particular risk of eye-related illnesses spreading more than usual. The Bhavishya Malika goes further, predicting the emergence of new, incurable diseases that could overwhelm healthcare systems and cause widespread panic."

"Moving on from the weather disasters to the man made ones. The border situation always seems tense. What do the predictions say about India-Pakistan and India-China?"

"The astrological and psychic consensus is that 2025 is a year of heightened military tension. Everything points to covert warfare, border skirmishes, and the risk of escalation with Pakistan. The May

2025 conflict was a direct response to terror attacks, and while a ceasefire is holding, the charts warn of further violations and the risk of renewed hostilities, especially in the disputed regions."

"And China?"

"The charts show continued tension along the border, with the risk of standoffs and covert operations, especially during the summer months. The psychic consensus is that India will be forced to take a more assertive stance, but open war is unlikely in 2025—though the risk rises sharply after 2027."

"What about the stock market and the economy?", trying to scribble some points quickly. I still had two major themes to cover after this one.

"The market is in for a wild ride. The period from March to July is flagged for sharp corrections, especially after July. The window from July to November is a classic marker for financial crisis or global recession, with warnings of debt tightening, unemployment spikes, and possible defaults in financial institutions. The advice from the stars and psychics: avoid risky bets, diversify, and keep some assets in gold or government-backed instruments. Unemployment is a growing concern. The psychic consensus is that 2025 is a year of stress and adaptation, with rising joblessness, social unrest, and a sense of fatigue from years of uncertainty. But there's also a strong theme of resilience and spiritual awakening—India is predicted to emerge as a global spiritual hub, with a renewed focus on community, tradition, and innovation."

"I have two more theme questions. Before we go there, any final words for India and Asia?"

"2025 is the start of a global crisis, with war, economic upheaval, and natural disasters acting as catalysts for a new era. A period where money and gold lose value, food becomes scarce. Channeled sources echo this, predicting a mass spiritual awakening, the rise of humanity beyond the past and a slow but steady shift toward a more compassionate, community-driven society."

Crypto

"**L**isa, I keep hearing that crypto is the future of money, but with all the wild swings, government crackdowns, and talk of digital currencies, I'm honestly confused. Is crypto really going to take over, or is it just another bubble waiting to pop?"

Lisa (smiling) replied, "That's the million-dollar question! There's a lot of hype, but also a lot of misunderstanding. Psychic and astrological predictions agree: 2025 is a year of extreme volatility, with both massive gains and gut-wrenching crashes. The first half of the year is marked by uncertainty—tariffs, wars, and regulatory drama keep the market on edge. But the real action comes in the last three months, when crypto could see exponential growth, especially for Bitcoin and major coins. Some forecasts put Bitcoin's year-end target between $140,000 and $230,000, with the biggest gains likely coming in a sudden, late-year surge. However, it is shortlived as well. 2025 as a 'reset year' for money. There's a strong theme of old systems breaking down—banks, fiat currencies, even gold losing their traditional roles. Crypto is seen as both a safe haven and a wild card. Some channeled sources say digital currencies will become the backbone of the new financial system, but only after a period of chaos and cleansing."

"Is the government going to kill crypto with regulation? And what about central bank digital currencies?"

"Regulation is a double-edged sword. In 2025, expect a wave of new rules—especially in the US, Europe, and Asia. Some psychics see this as a positive, bringing legitimacy and institutional money. Others warn of crackdowns, especially on privacy coins and unregulated exchanges. The financial crisis of 2025 will be the trigger for governments to roll out digital dollars, euros, and yuan. These will coexist with crypto, but there's a risk of increased surveillance and loss of financial privacy. The psychic advice? Diversify, stay nimble, and don't keep all your wealth in one system."

"But didn't you mention in our other engagement that there is a major monetary reset coming?". I was talking about our 2026-2035 book that we have been working on.

"All predictions point to a severe economic crisis just before a global war, with money and gold losing their value altogether. Prices of essentials skyrocket, and even food becomes hard to afford. The prophecy says the rich and poor become equal - which is a tough image to process. That is a conversation for another time."

I looked at my list. I had just one more question. AI.

AI and its Impact on Humanity

I slumped back in my chair, massaging my cramped hand. "Lisa, I think this is the first notepad I have ever actually finished in my life. If psychic predictions are right, my next investment should be in wrist braces."

Lisa laughed, setting her own pen down with a theatrical sigh. "If I'd known we'd cover this much ground, I'd have brought a backup notepad—and maybe a bottle of wine. But hey, at least we're making history for both of us!"

I flipped to a fresh page, determined to squeeze in one last topic. "Alright, before my hand gives out completely—let's talk about AI. I've seen so many headlines, but what do the psychics and astrologers actually say about specific AI incidents in 2025?"

Lisa grinned, eyes lighting up despite the long day. "You're in luck—this is one area where the predictions get surprisingly concrete. Here's what's coming up again and again in the forecasts and channeled messages."

"Lay it on me. I'll try to keep up."

"First, 2025–2026 is flagged for a wave of strict government action on AI. Psychics and channelers see major governments—especially the U.S.—rolling out tough new regulations. Think bans on unapproved AI, mandatory transparency for decision-making, and even an executive order that forces tech giants to share their AI safety secrets.

It's not just talk; the predictions say this will actually happen, and it'll shake up the whole tech world."

"So, not just more guidelines, but real, enforceable rules?"

"Exactly. And it's not just policy. The astrologers point to mid-2025—especially June and July—as a hotspot for AI-powered cyberattacks. There's a Mars–Saturn stress aspect then, which is classic for tech disruptions. Psychic sources warn of 'smart malware' that evolves on its own, targeting healthcare and aviation networks. We're talking about widespread outages, data breaches, and a real scramble to keep critical systems online."

"That sounds like a sci-fi movie. What about military stuff? Any predictions there?"

"Yes, and it's pretty wild. Channeled military analysts predict the first use of fully autonomous AI drones in a Middle Eastern conflict by late 2025. Astrologers tie this to July 20—a classic setup for sudden tech warfare breakthroughs. The concern is that this will raise huge ethical and security questions, and could even force a global debate about AI in warfare."

"And the markets? I keep hearing AI could cause another flash crash."

"That's right. Psychics foresee AI-driven trading algorithms triggering a global market flash crash in June–July 2025. The losses could top 5% in major indices before a rapid rebound. Financial astrologers blame Uranus in Taurus opposing Pluto—basically, a cosmic signal for disruptive tech overturning old financial systems."

"Is there any hope for society, or is it all chaos?"

"Actually, there's a silver lining. Channelers describe a 'collective awakening' around AI ethics. Jupiter's transit through Gemini in May 2025 is linked to public protests demanding that AI respect human rights. Psychic sources also predict grassroots 'AI literacy' movements—basically, people teaching each other how to spot AI bias and defend against manipulation."

I set my pen down, finally admitting defeat. "Well, Lisa, if the world doesn't end, at least I'll have a finished notepad to show for it. Maybe I'll frame it as a relic of the year AI went wild."

Lisa grinned, raising her tea in a mock toast. "To finished notepads, psychic predictions, and a future where we're just a little bit more prepared for whatever AI throws at us."

Dusk was settling over the foothills as I finally stood, stretching my legs and feeling the ache in my hand from a day's worth of furious note-taking. The sky was streaked with lavender and gold, the last light glinting off the peaks and filtering through the pines. Lisa looked as exhausted as I felt—her shoulders slumped, eyes reflecting both the weight of the world's predictions and the simple relief of a long day drawing to a close. She glanced at her phone, a gentle reminder that it was time for her to check in with her kids before another stretch of client meetings. These interviews always took her away from family, and I could sense her eagerness to return to that circle of warmth and laughter.

I thanked her, meaning it more than ever. "Lisa, I don't know how you do this—holding space for so many futures, so many worries. Thank you for your patience, your insights, and your humor. I think this is the first notepad I've ever actually filled front to back." We both laughed, a little weary, a little proud. I gave her a hug, feeling the familiar mix of gratitude and camaraderie that always came at the end of these sessions. "Go call your kids," I said. "You've more than earned it."

As I walked out to my car, the air was cool and sweet, the world quiet except for the distant call of a bird and the crunch of gravel beneath my shoes. Driving back toward the airport, I watched the mountains recede in the rearview mirror, their outlines softened by twilight. The road unwound before me, headlights flickering on as dusk deepened into night.

A sense of prophecy lingered in the silence—the feeling that we were all, in our own way, navigating a world on the brink of transformation. I thought of Lisa's words: turbulence, reckoning, awakening. The future was as uncertain as ever, but somehow, after a day of wrestling with predictions and possibilities, I felt less afraid. Maybe it was the comfort of patterns, or the hope that even in chaos, there are signals worth listening to. Or maybe it was just the knowledge that, whatever comes, we face it together—one conversation, one question, one finished notepad at a time.

As the city lights appeared on the horizon, I found myself smiling. The world might be unpredictable, but there's beauty in the mystery—and in the courage it takes to keep asking what comes next.

Other Predictions for 2025 discussed post April 2025

· Asia will be hotbed of activity and changes. India-Pakistan continued issues. A major country in South Asia, likely Pakistan, will cease to exist by 2027; another will see extended downturn from Feb 2026

· The two-state solution will be off the table by 2028 if not achieved by then

· Iran's current regime will change completely, with strong internal support for this change

· A protective new moon with Jupiter will prevent worst-case scenarios and buffer against all-out war. There will be temporary peace or ceasefire agreements, but these will not be permanent

· Event: "25 June" tipping point for destruction. If 25 June 2025 passes without ceasefire, 25 June–28 July period "very terrible," with nuclear-weapons risk rising dramatically

· Event: Global war escalation toward extended conflict especially towards September 2025 to 2027–28.

Multiple-country conflict evolving by September 2025, extending through 2027–28.

• Event: Blocking of Strait of Hormuz and energy crisis, expect blocking of the Strait of Hormuz, triggering real energy and power shortages.

• Event: June through 20 August 2025; heightened tension and potential bloodshed

• Event: China/Russia likely to join by proxy; Terrorist attacks and higher military/civilian casualty rates in armed forces

• Event: Starting mid July to October, Heavy—yet storage-deficient—monsoon rains, flooding, landslides, and failure of crop reserves globally in 2025.

• Event: Southern India cyclone and quakes; South India faces a "super cyclone" and earthquake risk in June–July 2025, plus northern hill-state floods and landslides; Intensified cyclone/hurricane activity in the Caribbean, Bay of Bengal, and Arabian Sea

• A localized disease outbreak (not a full pandemic) will occur in Asia

• Canada will experience wildfires less severe than California's but still noteworthy

• Surge in fire-related disasters, heatwaves, and underbrush ignition incidents, Undersea volcanic eruptions and tsunami threats, especially near tectonic zones; Solar flares disrupting communications, power grids, and satellite operations

· Breakthroughs in space exploration—new satellite missions or planetary discoveries

· Israel's June 2025 strike on Iran's nuclear program confirms prophetic timelines and inaugurates the foretold seven-year cycle of global upheaval spanning 2025–2032. In retaliation, Iran is expected to target U.S. and Israeli embassies as well as overseas bases, potentially employing sleeper cells, while bus and mass-transit terror attacks surge during peak commuting hours in Israel and allied nations. Large gatherings—stadiums, outdoor concerts, and other crowded venues—will become primary terror targets, and assassination plots against country leaders may be orchestrated under close Iranian intelligence surveillance. The threat landscape will escalate to include biological or radiological devices endangering urban centers such as Tel Aviv, and globalist actors could exploit peaceful protests to launch simultaneous "fear attacks". Heightened risk of tactical nuclear or radiological weapon use in strategic hotspots will endanger Western military personnel and diplomatic posts, while Syrian oil-field incendiary attacks underscore Syria's pivotal role in the broader Middle East conflict. Iraq and Kuwait are likely to be drawn into hostilities, triggering spikes in oil and gas prices, and massive refugee flows, civilian exoduses, and urban evacuations will mirror wartime migrations. Iran may attempt sea-launched missile strikes on coastal installations, weekend protest events worldwide could mask coordinated terror operations, and electromagnetic disruptions from solar storms may compound these man-made crises. Although a temporary peace pact might emerge within this seven-year framework, it is predicted to ultimately collapse.

Books by 26 Psychics

2025 - THE BIG BOOK OF Psychic Predictions
https://books2read.com/u/bxOEYo
2025 Numerology Predictions
https://books2read.com/u/b6qnr6
2025-2030 - Small Book of Psychic Predictions
https://books2read.com/u/4EgEYl